Administering the Elementary Band:

Teaching Beginning Instrumentalists and

Developing a Band Support Program

Administering the Elementary Band:

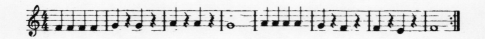

Parker Publishing Company, Inc.

Teaching Beginning Instrumentalists and Developing a Band Support Program

RUSSELL A. PIZER

West Nyack, N. Y.

Administering the Elementary Band:
Teaching Beginning Instrumentalists
and Developing a Band Support Program

by Russell A. Pizer

© 1971 BY

PARKER PUBLISHING COMPANY, INC.
WEST NYACK, N.Y.

LIBRARY OF CONGRESS
CATALOG CARD NUMBER: 72-155291

PRINTED IN THE UNITED STATES OF AMERICA
ISBN—0-13-004994-8
B&P

Dedicated to

Dr. William D. Revelli

...without whose inspiration I might have been content with the ordinary

ACKNOWLEDGMENTS

Most of the ideas in this book were used by me while teaching in the elementary school. In addition I have drawn freely upon the writings, surveys and research of others, and gratefully acknowledge them. The single greatest source I have used is *The Instrumentalist*. This magazine, published by Traugott Rohner and under the editorship of John Christie for a number of years, is a veritable encyclopedia for teaching instrumental music and a guide to developing that God-created art to which many of us have dedicated our lives—band music.

It would be impossible for me to decipher which ideas came directly from Dr. William D. Revelli or such others who have had a profound effect upon my life and teaching as George Cavender and the other members of the wind and percussion faculty at the University of Michigan.

My acknowledgments also go to Francis Byrne, the principal at Roscoe Conkling School in Utica, New York, where I taught for several years. It was through his understanding and excellent knowledge of music that he allowed me to develop a program much like the one set forth in this book.

What You Will Find in This Book

This book has grown out of the many questions, discussions, and experiences that I have had in establishing elementary bands, in depending on them as a high school band director, and in teaching about them in colleges. These aren't all the answers or the only answers, but this book does contain many answers and many approaches to almost all the problems that music educators will face in establishing, maintaining and improving the elementary band.

Chapter 1 includes four different approaches for successfully recruiting for the beginning elementary band. It covers the physical characteristics needed for each instrument and shows in detail how a teacher can influence students into the right selection.

The "Outline for Teaching the Clarinet to Beginners" in Chapter 2 is one of the most complete to ever appear in print. By following this step-by-step procedure, any teacher should be well on the way to producing excellent woodwind players. This procedure is adaptable to the teaching of all instruments.

Each of the eight chapters contains similarly proven and handy information that can be adapted to fit any elementary band program.

The emphasis in this book is on the administering of the various aspects of the program. Included in this book is not only the teachings of the various aspects of the elementary band program but also the many administrative details upon which hinges the ultimate success of the program.

This book, then, will help the band director establish an elementary instrumental curriculum in a step-by-step manner. Along with the establishment of the curriculum it gives the band director many ideas and alternatives on how to run the elementary band program efficiently and professionally.

Russell A. Pizer

Table of Contents

Administering the Elementary Band:

Teaching Beginning Instrumentalists and

Developing a Band Support Program

1

Initiating the
Elementary Band Program

PREPARATION FOR RECRUITING

The first steps in recruiting for the elementary band are to inform the students as to the feasibility of taking an instrument, what instruments are available and what is entailed in the pursuit of such an activity. Perhaps of even greater importance is to seek methods of creating enthusiasm and interest on the part of the students to take part in such a venture.

For those who are beginning a brand new band program or revitalizing an old one, the pre-band class, using such instruments as the song flute, flutophone, tonette, etc., can act as an effective catalyst to divert heretofore undiscovered musically talented children onto the rolls of the school bands. This pre-band class can create great enthusiasm for a future in the beginning band and lay a firm foundation in musical fundamentals that will apply directly to band instruments.

PRE-BAND PROGRAMS

There is considerable evidence that the best time to start a pre-band program is during the fourth grade. There have been a number of surveys on this question, each substantiating the fourth grade as an excellent starting point, saving the beginning band activities for the fifth grade.

The various aspects of the pre-band program will not be dealt with herein. The reader however is referred to several articles on the subject by this author. They include: "Fourth Grade Instrumental Program," *The Instrumentalist,* October, 1968; "Fourth Grade Instrumental Curriculum," *The Instrumentalist,* August, 1968; "Pre-band Instruments for Fourth Graders," *The Instrumentalist,* August, 1968; and "Toward More Accurate Rhythm," *The Instrumentalist,* September, 1968.

At the conclusion of the pre-band program or even if the pre-band program is not given, an excellent jumping-off point into the beginning band program is the giving of a musical aptitude test to all fourth graders. This should be administered at the very end of the school year.

APTITUDE TESTS

In examining and administering a musical aptitude test it is well to remember that no test yet devised can tell definitely how much success an individual will achieve in the study of music or how far he may go should he decide to take up the study of an instrument.

There will be students who will make relatively low grades yet will achieve much in this work while others may make high grades and not be so inclined to pursue the study of music. Therefore it should be understood that this is a test of natural ability only. Success will depend upon the effort put forth by the individual to develop his ability as applied and related to an instrument.

There are three important things that will govern the extent to which musical ability is developed. They are: interest, industry, and instruction.

A "gift of music" is very largely tied in with an *interest* in music. It has often been said: "Musical talent is 10% inspiration and 90% perspiration."

Even though the aptitude test does not give the total picture, this and a musical accomplishment test, along with the other knowledge a teacher may acquire while working with the children in a pre-band class, adds up to a considerable amount of evidence. Evidence of this type can be used either to encourage parents to allow their child to become a part of the beginning instrumental program or, in some cases, discourage parents because their child lacks apparent ability, knowledge and/or sincere interest.

Recommendations

If the school offers a pre-band program and gives an aptitude test at the end of the fourth grade, the band director has two points upon which to evaluate the child's possibilities for success: the test and the instrumental teacher's evaluations of the child's attitude and actions in the pre-band class situation. Two additional items can be added to this: the classroom teacher's evaluation and the general music teacher's evaluation.

A form can be made up and submitted to these persons. The principal may also be included if he has a knowledge of the children and their parents. This form would include the grades the children have accumulated to this point—the pre-band class grade, aptitude and accomplishment test grades. One column with three or four sub-columns would be headed: "recommended for further study." A check mark would indicate: "yes, I would recommend him," a question mark would indicate: "possibly." No mark would mean: "no, I do not recommend him."

The teacher's or principal's initials would be placed at the top of the column. Thus the instrumental teacher would know what these persons felt about the potentialities of each child if he were to enter the beginning instrumental program.

A word of explanation about these recommendations should

be given however. Even if a particular student had not done particularly well in the pre-band class, as will be shown by his grades, the general music teacher, classroom teacher and principal should not hesitate to recommend a particular child for continued study if they feel the experience in this group would be of value to the individual.

It is possible for a child to do well in the beginning instrumental program even if he did not previously show any potential or interest in music. This is not likely but it is possible, as anyone who has developed a program of this type will testify.

FINAL STEPS

Another bit of information should be imparted to the children before the final step into the beginning band program is taken. This may be started early in the pre-band program (if such a class is given) and continued throughout, sneaking the idea into the class work from time to time. The children, and later the parents, should be informed in various ways about the problems of the adaptability of some people to certain kinds of instruments. There is one published booklet by the Conn Corporation of Elkhart, Indiana, that points this out vividly. It is titled: *What Instrument Shall I Play*.

If the children are told this early in their contacts with the instrumental program and references are constantly made to this problem, they will come to accept the idea and be open to suggestions from the instrumental teacher when selections are to be made.

The instrumental teacher can put himself in the position much like that of a football coach. The football coach is the one who decides who plays what part on the team, not the parents and not the students. The coach selects the students best suited to be quarter-back, he selects the students best suited to be a guard, etc.

The final step should be to have an evening program to

which parents of recommended students are invited. This meeting is for both parents and students.

The evening program should disseminate the following information:

1. The value of instrumental study
2. Which instrument a child should play
3. The methods by which they can secure an instrument
4. The differences in the various grades of instruments
5. The course of study—not only on the beginning level but the advanced level as well—the total picture
6. How the classes are handled—do they miss regular subjects, do they come before school, do they come after school, is there a rotating lesson schedule, etc?
7. What has been called the "three-way partnership"
   a. the teacher's responsibility
   b. the parent's responsibility
   c. the student's responsibility

CONTACTING THE PARENTS

The following procedures can be carried on whether or not a pre-band class is part of the total instrumental program. Those who are contacted will depend upon the existing numbers in the program and just how effective a pre-band program might be.

If the program is going along well and sufficient numbers are already in the program, the instrumental teacher can be more selective. If the program is lacking in sufficient numbers, almost all the children's parents could be contacted.

Illustrations 1-2, 1-3, and 1-4 (found at the end of this chapter) are facsimiles of some information that could be sent to parents in connection with the beginning band program.

A time sheet for when each event is to take place will insure a smooth functioning of the recruiting procedure. One such form is published by the Conn Corporation (see Illustration 1-6). A copy of this should be given to all involved, including the principal of the school, the educational representative of the music store that may be handling the rental-purchase program, and possibly the classroom teachers whose students will be participating in the program.

Plan Number One

Mail a form letter to parents of the students who are considered eligible to join the beginning instrumental classes.

It is a good plan to call the meeting in a small room and then move to larger quarters if the attendance is large. It is quite discouraging to have fifteen or twenty parents in a large auditorium, while the same number in a classroom will seem like a good turn-out.

A telephone call or a flyer to each parent on the day of the meeting, to remind them to be present, will be found worthwhile. Illustration 1-5 is an example of such a flyer.

The telephone call could be made by someone other than the instrumental teacher and go something like this:

> Hello, Mrs. Smith. This is John Jones: I am calling for Mr. _____, the band director at school. No doubt you know that James (first name of son or daughter) took the music test the other day and passed very satisfactorily, and Mr. _____ is quite anxious to have him (her) in the band. He is wondering if you have given it any thought?

This provides an opportunity for the parent to enter the conversation with the result that many valuable points of information may be brought out. If the response has been favorable, the person phoning can close very nicely be saying:

> Well, Mr. _____ asked me to call and invite you personally to attend the meeting at the school tonight. He would like to have James come with you so that he can make sure whether or not he is physically able to play the instrument you might like for him to have.

If the parent seems interested, but for some reason cannot attend the meeting, the person calling might add that he will ask Mr. _____ to call her for a special appointment. In this case a sheet should be kept to refer the director to these persons.

If the telephone calls are made, the instrumental teacher has a fair idea of just how many he might expect at the meeting.[1]

Plan Number Two

Arrange the test card-records by streets and make calls at each home to interest the parents in allowing the son or daughter to become a member of the beginners' class. This gives the instrumental teacher an opportunity to use the information on the cards regarding the student. Frequently the parent will become interested enough in the test that they would like to take it also. It is well to have a few extra cards along and take time to give a part of the test with a piano, or one of the instruments in your car (or a transistorized tape recorder). It is well to have a few of the more popular instruments in the car; but do not make the mistake of taking an instrument into the house until you have definitely interested the parent.

It is easy to interest the parent of the students who have made good grades. Many points to convince the parents of those who have fallen below the line, that their child should study music, can also be given.

A prominent high school bandmaster in Wisconsin urged two students, who showed in various tests that they might possess the least natural ability in music, to enroll in his beginners' class. One of these students could not distinguish between tones on the piano unless the notes were more than an octave apart. The other could not walk at the cadence counted by the instructor and would invariably take four or six steps while five were being counted. It is a significant fact that both of these students developed into first chair players in less than four years.

---

[1]Howard Lyons, *Recruiting the School Band and Orchestra* (Elmhurst, Illinois: Lyons Band Instrument Co., 1959), 19.

It is likewise true that this type test will show great musical tendencies in some students. If these students are interested in music they will, quite naturally, develop into outstanding players with less effort, and in a shorter time, than their less musically inclined classmates.

It is also true that the test gives very definite information regarding the strong and weak tendencies of the students. Students who are weak in rhythm should be given special work to overcome this handicap, as all people use rhythm in almost every action.

All sports such as golf, tennis, skating, etc., demand the use of rhythm and even work such as typing, driving a car or digging a ditch can be done better if done in rhythm.

Weakness in hearing or in distinguishing between tones should be overcome. In many cases this is carelessness in listening and lack of concentration. If the student is weak in melodic recognition this undoubtedly should be developed, since accurate hearing is necessary in every walk of life and musical training will do more to help a person toward accurate and thoughtful listening than any other study.

Plan Number Three

A telephone campaign based on the list of names on the test cards will reap a fair crop of new members.

The purpose of the call is to make a definite appointment for the organizer to see the parent at the home. The person making the calls should have a full knowledge of the problems at hand and should have visited at least one of the classrooms while the testing was being given. It will be well for the persons making these calls to alter the wording to suit their own particular style so that it will sound "natural," and will suit local conditions.

A typical telephone dialogue:

Mrs. Jones, I am calling in the interest of the new beginners' class that Mr. Brown (the director) is organizing at the Franklyn school. As you perhaps know, a test was given in the school recently to determine the natural musical ability of the students. Your son, John, made a very acceptable grade and we are wondering if you had considered allowing him to join the school band?

At this point you will get some sort of response and the conversation from this point will be determined by the response.

Needless to say the voice should be cheerful, interesting, and above all things, easily understood. The person making these telephone calls should rehearse the speech until it flows easily; but should avoid allowing it to sound mechanical. Clear enunciation of the words is very important—and remember, the person listening knows nothing of the test or plan for a beginners' group.

The house calls following this will be much the same as in Plan Number Two with the exception that the parents will be expecting the instrumental teacher, and already will have admitted their interest.

The person making the telephone calls has but one thing to do and that is to secure a definite appointment for the instrumental teacher. Any questions over the phone should be answered, of course, but avoid giving any misinformation or indicating any hesitancy because either may possibly lose a good band prospect.[2]

Combining the Three Plans

If Plan Number One is used, those children who got exceptionally good grades but whose parents do not attend the meeting could be called upon at their home. This especially should be done if the instrumental teacher is aware the children are interested in joining the band. Perhaps the parents just do not come to school for anything, least of all a meeting about learning to play a band instrument. These home calls are necessary and important if the father or mother or both work an evening

---

[2]*Conn Music Aptitude Test* (Oak Brook, Illinois: C. G. Conn Ltd., 1938), p. 20.

shift. Perhaps these parents could be encouraged to come to school for a meeting with the instrumental teacher during the day if there were enough interested persons.

TEACHER AIDS

A portion of this work could be handled by other persons besides the instrumental teacher. The telephone calls could be a yearly project for the band parents' club. The calls to the homes of parents who did not come to the meeting could be done by the instrument company's educational representative. Be sure, however, that the school officials are sure he will not force the parents into taking an instrument.

Having someone other than the instrumental teacher make the telephone calls prevents the problem of the parents asking too many questions over the telephone that should be taken care of during the home visit. If members of the band parents' club do this task, the parent on the other end of the telephone will be very likely to listen. This in turn gives the instrumental teacher apparent support from other parents.

NEWSPAPER AID

The local newspaper can also aid in developing interest in the beginning band program. Some examples of possible news articles are shown in Illustration 1-1[3].

THE INTERVIEW

The next step will depend upon the number of parents that attend the evening program. This number can be fairly well

---

[3]Lyons, p. 18.

ILLUSTRATION 1-1

RENTAL INSTRUMENTS AVAILABLE FOR NEW SCHOOL BAND

With the intention of recruiting a large number of students for the school band, Bandmaster _____ has announced that all students will be given an opportunity to enroll in new band to be formed in the near future.

While conferring with Superintendent _____ the decision was reached that all students would be tested with a scientific test to check their musical ability, and that arrangements would be made whereby instruments could be rented for three months to determine the instrument best suited to each individual child and his' interest in it. This method of starting children on musical instruments is being widely used by schools throughout the country with great success.

Lessons will be furnished by the school. Now is the logical time for children to start, and it will only be a matter of months before they will be given an opportunity to win a chair in the regular band and to participate in all of the school band functions.

MANY EAGER TO JOIN NEW SCHOOL BAND

Enthusiasm Runs High As Future Sousas Enroll

With the enthusiasm that only youth can display, many boys and girls are accepting the invitation to "Join the Band" offered by the _____ schools.

The opportunity of obtaining an instrument on the rental plan is largely responsible for the interest being taken by parents and pupils in the program. "It looks as though our quota will be reached very soon," commented Mr. _____, the Director, the morning after the display and Meeting held in the school last Wednesday, Mr. _____ also stated that any parent not able to attend that Meeting may still obtain all the necessary information about joining the group if he will contract him at the school or at his home.

NEW BAND TO BE RECRUITED IN SCHOOLS

Sixty new recruits for the new school band is the objective of the campaign which will begin soon in the schools of _____.

"It is not impossible to achieve this goal," says Bandmaster _____.

All parents desire their children to play some musical instruments, and the schools offer the best opportunity for them to do so. Unfortunately, every child is not naturally adapted to playing a musical instrument. In order to determine those best suited to participate, scientific tests will be given to determine the inherent musical ability of the children Arrangements will be made whereby instruments may be rented for three months to make sure the children will succeed before further investment is made. Parents whose children successfully pass the test will be notified.

BAND INSTRUMENT DISPLAY WEDNESDAY NIGHT

Parents and Students May View All Types Used in Band and Orchestra

New band and orchestra instruments will be on display at the _____ Wednesday evening of this week. Parents and school children are cordially invited by the Band Director to see the exhibit.

This exhibit is held in conjunction with a meeting of parents and pupils who have been invited to join the new instrumental classes just being formed.

To furnish the best data on the possible success of a boy or girl, music tests were given to all children from the Fourth Grade through the Ninth Grade a few days ago. Parents whose children did exceptionally well were so advised by the Director.

An interesting talk regarding the functions of each type of instrument will be given by an expert on band instruments, and the educational advantages of each will be explained. The method of obtaining an instrument on the rental plan to further check the child's ability will be explained in detail.

determined by asking the children to return a notice from their parents or the telephone responses.

The actual signing up of the children should be done in a relaxed, quiet atmosphere so the parent will feel free to ask any further questions he may have about the program. At the conclusion of the evening's demonstration, a large chart can be placed in the hall outside the room where the meeting is being held for parents to sign up for personal interviews.

These interviews will be held at school between the parent, the child, the instrumental teacher and, if an instrument company is used for rentals, their representative. It is during this time that a child is actually assigned an instrument and fees paid.

A procedure like this places a great deal of importance on the personal approach and parents come to see this as a professionally run and operated setup. They see that their child will be treated individually and each parent will have full knowledge of what is going on. They will see that their child receives every benefit from this profitable experience and that all questions are answered to their satisfaction and are not shoved into taking one of "those crazy horns" home that is going to cost them a fortune.

ADAPTATION

An intermediate step might be taken between the parent program and the interviews. There could be established an interval of a few weeks between the parent program and the interviews to allow for an exploratory class in the adaptation of the children to the instruments. Though it is possible to predict with a good deal of accuracy which instrument is best for a child, an actual period where experimentation can be done on the various instruments would make for a more careful and accurate selection.

ADAPTATION CLASSES[4]

At the first meeting of the adaptation classes, every pupil registered for beginning instrumental class instruction should be present. Up to this time no definite instrument has been assigned. One of the first processes of classification, perhaps, is that of determining which students seem best adapted to brass instruments.

The instructor may choose to take the cornet first as the specific instrument on which he will attempt to determine adaptabilities. He begins by demonstrating, or having one of the better players in the high school band demonstrate, the possibilities, qualities, functions, general position, and sound of the cornet. After such a demonstration, he explains briefly some of the elements of brass playing, stressing the importance of lip vibration and breath control.

Class Exercises

The entire class is asked to participate in an exercise. Each pupil places his lips so that they are very much relaxed, or "loose," and away from the teeth. Then he blows his breath outward between the teeth in such a way that lips are set into vibration, causing a sound which can be described as similar to the "putter" of a motor boat. By demonstrating and asking for the sound of the "putter," the instructor usually elicits the desired response.

This simple exercise tends to relax the lip muscles and encourages participation by all students, including the timid or self-conscious. As the children take part in the exercise, the instructor observes the facial characteristics of the various students. It is at this point that he studies the child's jaw, teeth,

---

[4]The following, through page 34, is from William D. Revelli, "Basic Qualities Viewed in Adaptation Classes." *The Instrumentalist*, VI, 6, (May-June, 1952), 16.

lips, muscle strength, and general qualifications. After a few minutes of this exercise, it is advisable to move quickly about the room, testing each child individually on his ability to "putter." It will be amazing to find that some students are quite flexible in performance of the exercise while others have the greatest difficulty with it.

If the instructor makes a note of which pupils can "putter" easily, he has a start toward classification. He has at least an idea of which children can be assigned to the brass family. Although a child's inability to perform this exercise properly is not a definite proof of his being unable to play a brass instrument, there is at any event an indication of prospective brass players.

Since the "putter" exercise does not require the type of lip vibration necessary to the playing of a brass instrument, the next step would be that of beginning actual lip vibration. This exercise would be conducted by asking the children to place the lips in a position slightly touching each other in the manner of a pucker or a whistling position. The breath is then blown between the lips, producing a vibration with a resultant sound very similar to the buzzing of a bee.

The "buzz" exercise, it must be realized, is far more intricate than the "putter" exercise. There are many teaching technics that must be observed in the proper performance of this exercise. Many teachers permit the children to place their lips too firmly together, not realizing that a too firm position causes inflexibility and that through tightening of the lips a strain and rigidity occur in the muscles of the throat and chin.

Common Fault

Another common fault at this stage is the permitting of the "red" of the lips to be pursed out too far. When the lips are in the proper position, the "red" of the lips is turned under. The lips, though only touching each other, should be puckered away from the teeth. The lips do not change their position while the breath is being blown between them; absence of strain is combined with ease of performance. Properly begun, this vibration can be attained with little more effort than the pupil would ordinarily use to hum or whistle. It is constant over-exertion at this stage that causes so much tense, rigid playing at a later stage of the child's training.

The amount of progress made and the time spent on these exercises will be determined, naturally, by the number of children enrolled and the length of the class period. In any case, however, ultimate good results must depend on the thoroughness and care given to the first few "lessons." Usually, if given at all, these preliminary endeavors are too hurried. The classes should meet for at least three periods of not less than thirty minutes each, depending upon the size of the class.

Ordinarily, the first class period concludes with the "putter" exercise, collectively and individually given. The second session concludes with everyone having had the opportunity to "buzz," both individually and collectively. If the class is large, an added session is recommended rather than rushing over these important phases of class problems. At the end of the second, or "buzz" session, the instructor will have recorded the names of those pupils who show adaptation for instruments of the brass family. By this time there will be a number of children showing little or no aptitude for these instruments.

Mouthpiece Used

The next step will be that of testing the class, both individually and as an ensemble, with cornet mouthpieces. Each child should have an opportunity to vibrate his lips against the mouthpiece. The instructor should be sure to advise the child to avoid pressure and to practice a relaxed easy manner of "buzzing." It will be found that some children who were unable to "buzz" before using the mouthpiece are now able to produce a satisfactory vibration; they should be considered as prospective brass players.

Other factors involved in adaptation to brass playing include evenness of teeth and a certain texture of lip and type of face muscles. Usually the instructor must avoid assigning the cornet to those children having extremely short upper or lower teeth, a decided underslung jaw, or weak lip muscles. Rugged heavy lips, square jaws, long even teeth, and sufficient "red of the lip" to provide a cushion usually indicate the embouchure and facial characteristics conducive to good brass playing.

Those having unusually heavy lips with more than average "red" are prospective trombone, baritone, and tuba players. Naturally, in transferring pupils from a cornet group to one of the other brass instrument groups, the instructor must consider mental quickness, strength, size, general attitude, and interest of the child being shifted.

Decisions Reached

If we are operating on an adequate schedule, we shall find at the end of the third adaptation lesson that we have reached certain decisions. First, we have temporarily selected the children for the cornet classes. Second, we have listed those pupils assigned to cornet classes who, in view of adaptation tests, will later be transferred to other instruments of the brass family. Because of their age and size in this grade, they would not as yet be able to perform on the larger brass instruments.

Third, we have temporarily eliminated from these cornet classes those students showing no adaptation for that instrument and have tentatively assigned them to one of the three remaining groups of instruments.

All pupils enrolled in beginning classes will likewise attend the woodwind adaptation class, where for the time being all are considered students of the clarinet. It is the clarinet which serves as the trial instrument for determination of woodwind adaptation.

Adaptation for Woodwinds

The problems of physical adaptation for woodwind instruments are far less numerous than those of the brass family. This is especially true in the matter of embouchure, as there are many more requirements for brass embouchures. While the teeth, type of lip, jaw formation, etc., all have some effect upon the playing of woodwinds, they do not influence performance to the same extent that they do brass performance. Other characteristics which must be observed include the fingers, especially in regard to length, thickness, agility, and dexterity. These factors are of special importance to the woodwind beginner.

Embouchure Control

The child should be given a clarinet mouthpiece with a satisfactory reed carefully adjusted. From the child's placement of the mouthpiece the instructor can judge lip position, control, and embouchure in general. After the third session in this group, just as in the brass classes, those children who are best adapted for clarinet can be listed, including those who will later be transferred to other instruments in the woodwind family.

There is little need, perhaps, for discussing in detail the procedures to be followed in testing adaptability to the percussion group. In each case a procedure similar to the one outlined above, with appropriate equipment and attention to physical and mental requirements, will bring about the desired results.

Every child should be given an opportunity to take tests for adaptation in each of the three groups. It is quite possible that some children are versatile enough to do well in all. In such cases, a great deal more attention should be given to the child's desire about the instrument he prefers to play. Instructors should never assign certain instruments to students simply with the idea that they will thereby achieve balance of instrumentation for their organizations. In every case actual adaptability of the youngster should be the criterion for assignment. Experience has shown that nature provides enough differences in children to give the instructor an evenly balanced organization.

An instructor who carefully follows the adaptability procedures outlined will find that the problem of correct proportions, as well as correct apportions, will solve itself. Psychological problems which one meets with beginning pupils who have certain notions about what instruments they wish to play usually resolve themselves when the informed instructor carefully permits the student and his parents to know that there is a great deal more to the selection of an instrument than just choosing one because of its appearance or popular appeal.

A sane logical approach to the matter of adaptability will eliminate many of the weaknesses in our present programs and will strengthen the whole course of music progress.

PHYSICAL CHARACTERISTICS FOR EACH INSTRUMENT

Flute

1. Choose a child whose arms are long enough to hold the flute easily to his mouth and at the same time cover the keys correctly with the fingers.
   a. If the arms are too short for the long stretch, it will tend to make the embouchure lopsided.
   b. The little finger of the left hand should be able to reach the G-sharp key.
2. Lips should generally tend to be of smooth texture and not too thick.
   a. A bead on the upper lip is a great detriment to successful playing of the flute.
3. A very small mouth is often not as easily adjusted because of too short an upper lip.
4. Even teeth are an advantage.
5. During adaptability classes the student should be able to easily produce a tone on the head joint alone after some instruction in embouchure formation.
   a. The child should be able to produce a strong, clear tone with the end of the head joint closed and open.

Oboe

1620456

1. The prospective player should have some musical background on another woodwind instrument before attempting the oboe.
2. Both upper and lower lip should be able to cover the teeth easily by curling them over the edge of the teeth.
3. Teeth that are to be covered by the lips should be smooth, even and free from sharp edges.
4. The teeth, when closed, should meet as evenly as possible with no protrusion of the lower jaw.
5. The individual should have short fingers which do not have to be cramped when holding the instrument and fingers wide enough to cover the tone holes easily.
6. The prospective oboist should lean toward the tendency of an extrovert, who likes to become an individual and not part of the flock.
7. Due to the necessity of a fine oboist manufacturing his own reeds, one should be slightly mechanically inclined and have considerable manual dexterity.[5]

Bassoon

1. The prospective player should have some musical background on another woodwind instrument before attempting the bassoon.
2. Same as the oboe.
3. Same as the oboe.
4. The student should have a moveable lower jaw so it can be underslung or recessed for forming the embouchure.
   a. A student with an overbite is an excellent prospect for the bassoon.
5. Long fingers are necessary for the covering of the tone holes. They should also be somewhat fleshy.

---

[5]Arthur Saam Best, *The Oboe and the English Horn*, (Oak Brook, Illinois: C. G. Conn Ltd., 1958) 3.

a. The child should be able to place the left thumb on the whisper key and easily reach and securely cover the *C* tone hole with the third finger.

Clarinet

1. The student must be physically large enough so that he may hold the instrument with the proper hand position and cover the tone holes properly.
   a. The little fingers of both hands must be able to reach their E/B keys.
2. Any student with normal teeth, lip and chin formation can play the clarinet successfully.
   a. Excessively thick lips, thin lips; overbite, underbite; or crooked teeth can all be compensated for.
   b. Sharp or jagged lower teeth should be guarded against.
   c. The two front teeth should protrude the same distance.
3. Natural aptitude for the clarinet may be determined by the student being able to produce a tone on the mouthpiece and barrel equal to *F* or *F-sharp*—first space on the treble clef.

Brass

1. Ability to buzz the lips.
2. Straight, even teeth with strong lip muscles.
   a. Protruding teeth would be a hindrance.
3. Thin lips are best suited for playing small mouthpiece instruments like the trumpet and French horn.
4. Heavier lips are best suited for playing larger mouthpiece instruments like the baritone, trombone and tuba.

Trombone

1. In addition to the above an arm long enough to reach the lower positions is a necessity.

PARENT CONTACT

Illustrations 1-2, 1-3, 1-4, 1-5 and 1-6 are some examples of information that can be -sent home to parents from the outset to the conclusion of this beginning band program.

ILLUSTRATION 1-2[6]

Dear Parents:

Musical training is available for your child in the school band or orchestra which is being organized at the present time. Have you given any thought to this important phase of his education?

The child who learns to play an instrument learns discipline, cooperation with others, and a new way to a fuller, richer life. An instrument automatically places him in worthwhile school activities; it gives him something interesting, pleasurable and worthwhile to do during his leisure time.

As a result of a musical aptitude test recently given to pupils in the grade schools, recommendations for instrumental music training are being made. This method of discovering talent is proving successful wherever it is used, since only those boys and girls who can recognize rhythm and pitch are encouraged to take up the study of certain instruments.

We have made special arrangements with the educational Department of a reliable music company to aid you in obtaining an instrument on a THREE MONTHS' RENTAL PLAN. You may choose any instrument you wish. Your child may try it for three months under this plan. At the end of that time you may return it without further obligation, or you may keep it, the money already paid applying on its purchase, and easy monthly payments being arranged for the balance, if you so desire.

A MEETING of the PARENTS and PUPILS INTERESTED will be held in the _____ ON _____ AT _____
                (place)   (date)   (time)

ALL types of instruments will be on display and you will have a chance to confer with the director concerning the future musical education of your child.

                    Sincerely yours,

                    _____

Please return this questionnaire immediately.
- -
I am interested in my child joining the band or orchestra:
      YES_____ NO_____

My child is interested in playing _____ (instrument)

Pupil's Name _____   Parent's Name _____

School _____   Address _____

Grade _____   Phone _____

I will attend the Parents' meeting: YES _____ NO _____

---

[6]Lyons, page 16

ILLUSTRATION 1-3

CONKLING
SCHOOL
BAND

Dear Parent:

Musical training is available for your child in
the school band which is being organized at the
present time. Have you given any thought to this
important phase of your child's education?

The child who learns to play an instrument learns discipline, cooperation with others, and a new way to a
fuller, richer life. An instrument automatically places
him in a worthwhile school activity; it gives him something interesting, pleasurable and worthwhile to do
during his leisure time.

We have made special arrangements with the Educational Representative of a reliable music company to aid you in obtaining
an instrument on a rental plan. You may choose any instrument
you wish. Your child may try it for the rental period under
this plan. At the end of that period you may return it without further obligation, or you may keep it, the money already
paid applying on its purchase, and easy monthly payments being
arranged for the balance, if you so desire.

A MEETING OF THE PARENTS and PUPILS INTERESTED will be held at
CONKLING SCHOOL, THURSDAY evening SEPTEMBER 26th at 7:30 P.M.
in the School Auditorium. At this time we will answer any and
all questions you may have about our instrumental music program.

Sincerely,

Russell A. Pizer

Russell A. Pizer, Dir.

ILLUSTRATION 1-4

Student _____ _____
                                                Signature

Dear Parent:

It is my pleasure to inform you that your child _____ is now
eligible to start instruction on a musical instrument.

In an interview he she expressed a desire to play _____.

Registration will be complete when this letter is returned with the
parent's signature. All signed letters must be turned in to me by
_____.

FOR STUDENTS WHO DO NOT HAVE INSTRUMENTS

For those students who do not have instruments we have available a trial-
purchase plan through Peate's Music House in Utica. This is how the plan
works:

1. Your child needs a _____.

2. Trial fee for _____ weeks is _____.

3. If at the end of _____ weeks your child has made good progress,
   and you as parents and I as the teacher agree that there will be continued interest, the instrument may be purchased with the trial fee
   deducted from the original price of the instrument.

4. If, however, we are not convinced that your child is capable of complete success on the instrument, it may be returned at no further
   charge.

5. If you decide to purchase the instrument, terms for payment may be
   arranged with Peate's Music House.

To insure that the beginning students have their instruments by _____
(the first lesson day for beginners) we have arranged a meeting for all
parents of beginning students to be held in the _____ on
_____ at _____. At this time a representative of
Peate's Music House will be present with the necessary instruments. You
may pay the trial fee at this time and receive the instrument. Any
questions you may have about the program will be answered at this time.

Very truly yours,

Music Instructor

ILLUSTRATION 1-5

Dear Parent:

I want to remind you of the meeting for parents of beginning
students in the instrumental music program.

        TIME: _____

        PLACE: _____

A representative of Peate's Music House will be there with the
instrument for _____. The trial fee is _____
for _____ weeks and is to be paid when you receive the
instrument.

                    Very truly yours,

                    Music Instructor

ILLUSTRATION 1-6

CONN BAND RECRUITING PROGRAM
RECRUITMENT SCHEDULE SHEET
NOTE: TO BE COMPLETED BY BANDMASTER AND DEALER AT INITIAL PLANNING MEETING.

NAME OF SCHOOL _____

ADDRESS _____

CITY _____ STATE _____

BAND DIRECTOR _____

OR OTHER SCHOOL ADMINISTRATOR
HANDLING BAND RECRUITMENT PROGRAM _____ POSITION _____

TIME TABLE (NOTE FILL IN NO 5 DATE FIRST THEN FILL IN OTHERS)

1 INITIAL PLANNING MEETING	DATE _____	6 INSTRUMENTS TO BE DELIVERED	DATE _____
2 CONN APTITUDE TEST OR CONN WISIP TEST TO STUDENTS	DATE _____ (7 10 DAYS BEFORE PRESENTATION DATE)	7 "FUN, FUN, FUN" BOOKLET TO STUDENTS	DATE _____ (3 WEEKS AFTER INSTRUMENT DELIVERY TO STUDENTS)
3 INVITATION LETTER TO PARENTS INCLUDING BOOKLET "ENRICHED LIFE FOR YOUR CHILD THROUGH MUSIC"	DATE _____ (5 6 DAYS BEFORE PRESENTATION DATE)	8 BAND DIRECTOR "PROGRESS REPORT" TO PARENTS	DATE _____ (4 WEEKS AFTER INSTRUMENT DELIVERY TO STUDENTS)
4 NEWSPAPER ANNOUNCEMENT (OPTIONAL)	DATE _____ (2 DAYS BEFORE PRESENTATION DATE)	9 DEALER LETTER TO PARENTS	DATE _____ (3-4 WEEKS AFTER INSTRUMENT DELIVERY TO STUDENTS)
5 PRESENTATION DATE EXPLANATION OF BAND PROGRAM AND PLAN TO PARENTS AND STUDENTS	DATE _____	10 MUSIC PARENTS CLUB LETTER	DATE _____ (2-5 WEEKS AFTER INSTRUMENT DELIVERY TO STUDENTS)

PRESENTATION

LOCATION OR PLACE TO BE HELD	SCHOOL OFFICIALS ATTENDING
TIME	ANTICIPATED NUMBER OF PARENTS AND STUDENTS

MATERIALS NEEDED
TO SERVE THIS SCHOOL'S TOTAL PRESENTATION PROGRAM   (DEALER USE HANDY REPLY ORDER CARDS)

DESCRIPTION	QUANTITY	DESCRIPTION	QUANTITY
CONN APTITUDE TESTS		BOOKLET "AN ENRICHED LIFE FOR YOUR CHILD THROUGH MUSIC"	
CONN WISIP TESTS		BOOKLET "FUN, FUN, FUN"	
ENVELOPES "AN IMPORTANT MESSAGE FROM YOUR CHILD'S BAND DIRECTOR"		BOOKLET "THE MUSIC PARENTS CLUB"	
INTERVIEW CARDS		MUSIC STUDENT PERFORMANCE FILES	
FILM (NAME)		MUSIC STUDENT PRACTICE RECORDS	

BAND DIRECTOR'S COPY

2

Developing the Beginning
Band Program

The beginning band program is divided into class lessons, solo playing, technic class and beginning band. Each part of the program has a specific purpose, all leading to the development of the individual into a well-rounded instrumentalist.

Not to minimize the importance of the band rehearsal, but in this phase of the training program it serves only as the culmination of efforts put forth by instrumentalists. It also helps keep pupils interested, points out the deficiencies in their abilities and at the same time gives pupils a reason for work in the other areas of the program. Each band program must have as its cardinal aim improvement of the individuals' technical and musical abilities. If the program provides only band rehearsals, there will be very little real individual improvement. A band does not progress in proportion to the amount of time *they* rehearse. The band improves almost in direct proportion to the amount of time which is devoted to the improvement of the *individual* within the band through class lessons, solo playing and technic classes.

LESSON STRUCTURES

The first consideration to be given to a beginning band program is the structure within which the children are given their instrumental lessons. Only secondary is the setup of band rehearsals. It is advisable at the very outset that the children not immediately be placed in a large ensemble like a band. Only after they have achieved some degree of success at playing their instruments should this be attempted.

The method to be most highly recommended is that in which six children playing like instruments are met as a group. The lesson should last for thirty to forty-five minutes. Though it would be advisable to meet the children more than once a week at the outset, after a month of study, one meeting per week will suffice. This is because it will take a week for the children to successfully work out an assignment. More lessons within a week would only mean that the teacher helps the children practice the lesson and relieves the child of the personal responsibility of working out the material on his own.

At first view it might be considered far better to teach beginners in private lessons as the teacher could devote his entire energy to one individual. This however, is not the best answer to the question since other items must be considered when the child begins. These other factors are perhaps more important if considered from the overall viewpoint.

CLASS LESSONS

Class lessons are not only economical and effective, but the group spirit fostered by them can be of great importance. In a class the student learns to work with others and to play as a member of a group. He learns to compare pitches and tone quality, the importance of rhythmic accuracy and precision in the ensemble. From the beginning he learns what it takes to be a good member of the band.[1]

Children are familiar with classroom procedures and discipline in their regular school work. The individual lesson sepa-

[1]Fred Weber, "The Elementary and Junior High School Band Program," *Building Better Bands.* (Rockville Centre, L.I., N.Y.: Belwin-Mills Pub. Corp., 1957), 4.

rates a child from his friends. Alone he faces the teacher. Although the teacher may be tactful and sympathetic, it is psychologically impossible to create the same atmosphere that naturally exists in a class of several children.

Through the class lesson, the pupils develop self-confidence by being called upon to play by themselves from time to time. Many a mother has heard her child play perfectly but later exhibit extreme shyness or refuse to play at all when there are visitors present. "Nervousness" and "stage fright," so frequently the unsought byproduct of the private lesson, has no chance to develop in the class situation. The pupils in the class come to perform easily and naturally in the presence of others.[2]

Economy of motion for the teacher is another important factor when considering class lessons. The teacher explains the technic once and conserves the time for six separate explanations. A class lesson allows for children to ask questions that may be plaguing the others. It gives the children a group of friends who are in the same boat, a group of friends who can suffer along with each other. In the first stages these children do suffer trying to get that "thing" together, getting the reed on and all those terrible squeaks. Just where does that slide go for third position? No—that's too low—now you're too high! Which note is it supposed to be—G—no, lip is too tight—loosen up—no—you got tigheter, now you are playing the third space *C*, etc., etc.

If the teacher plays for a child in a private lesson, the child may become frustrated because he just cannot make his instrument sound like that of the teacher. In the class lesson the teacher can call upon certain individuals who represent examples of good tone quality, intonation, or embouchure. Those more proficient in the class can be called upon to demonstrate the application of many items being taught.

The spirit of competition is always good and does exist in a small way in the class lesson. Competition is the basis and life

[2]Otto W. Miessner, "The Piano Class Movement." *Yearbook of the Music Supervisors National Conference.* (Chicago: Music Supervisors National Conference, 1931), 248.

blood of our free enterprise system. Though not intended to be a competitive type of activity, nevertheless the class lesson does contribute to the healthy attitude of one child working in relation with others in the class and comparing his abilities with the abilities of the others.

The two greatest drawbacks with the class lesson setup are that the teacher cannot give full attention to an individual and his problems and the fact that everyone must move at the pace of the class. Those who do progress faster than the class must re-peat and sometimes re-repeat the same materials until the rest of the class has acquired the appropriate skills. This problem can partially be overcome by giving special assignments to the more advanced players, such as solos from a special solo book or supplementary exercises in other books. The progress of the class has to be geared to the average majority. This results in holding back the faster students but also may further confuse the slower ones.

Large groups of students are not always as well prepared for a lesson as a single private student. It is not unusual to have one or two come to the lesson with an instrument that is in need of minor adjustment or repair. If the instructor has a simple knowledge of the construction of the different instruments and can spare a few minutes at the start of each lesson to correct these difficulties with the aid of a handy repair kit, he will find that by the end of the year there have been fewer drop-outs than anticipated, and much valuable time will have been saved.[3]

INSTRUMENTS TO USE

Classes are easily set up with from four to as many as eight because only a few different kinds of instruments should be used in the fifth grade beginning program. The instruments herein are selected because of size and ease of playability by

[3]Robert J. Baasch, "On the Problems of Group Instruction," *Woodwind World*, IV, 2, (September, 1961), 14.

fifth graders. Too often a band director will put into the hands of a small child an instrument that he cannot play because of the size of his hand, fingers and/or arm. Even a clarinet is quite a large instrument for many a fifth grader, as is the trombone's slide.

The instruments to be recommended for the begining program are: flutes, clarinets, cornets, trombones, euphoniums, *E-flat* tubas and percussion. The more unusual instrument like the oboe, bassoon and even saxophones should be placed in the hands of sixth or seventh graders after they have had some previous training on the basic instruments.

For those desiring to play the French horn it is wise to begin on an alto horn, unless the child is of sufficient size to allow him to easily hold the French horn in the proper position and approach the mouthpiece easily at the correct angle. In some cases horn teachers allow a slight alteration in the position of the bell for the first few months of playing without undue damage being permanently set in the embouchure and position.

Not allowing children to start on the saxophone prevents the problem of ending up with ten or fifteen saxophones in the band and only five or six clarinets. Those making excellent progress on the clarinet could be given the opportunity of switching to saxophones after a period of time.

Drummers are usually a "problem" in a band rehearsal because they are just that—drummers! The solution to this problem is not to start "drummers," but "percussionists." At the very outset the students are percussionists because they should begin on some form of a keyboard instrument as well as a practice pad. Several percussion manufacturing companies are producing kits which include not only a snare drum, practice pad and sticks but also a rather inexpensive xylophone. Psychologically this gives the parents of a child more interest and allows the pupil in band to perform scales and warm-up studies on the xylophone along with other band members. It also prepares him for reading something other than just rhythm. Many a drummer upon reaching high school has no idea of how to play other percussion instruments like the timpani because he has never read pitches before.

By careful selection and transfer, the band from the sixth grade up can be well balanced. Thus an overbalanced organization like one that ends up with fifteen saxophones, ten clarinets, twenty-four cornets, ten trombones and nothing else will be alleviated.

This may seem like an unfair practice, but a balanced band is a desirable, if not a necessary thing. It is necessary to have balanced ensembles in the lower grades so that all the parts written by the composer are covered. The elementary basketball team does not use ten or twelve or thirteen children if they happen to be around. The elementary coach selects his first team from all those in his gym classes. So too, should the band director select those from his classes who perform the best to play on this first team—the band!

The problem of this type of selectivity is solved if the band director keeps this in mind and begins laying the foundation for this concept early in the instructional period. This point is also to be stressed to parents whenever the opportunity arises.

Administrators can be shown the validity of this method when comparing the band to the athletic teams even though it is important that everyone be given an opportunity to participate. If the program is successful, there are sufficient numbers to have *two* bands—the first, a select group, and the second an intramural-type group where anyone, whatever his ability, might participate. In some instances this second group might be made up of only ten or fifteen players. This still allows for the first band to be a select group.

Even most fifth graders can list the various positions on basketball, football and baseball teams. If they also knew the number and combinations of instruments in a band (a well-balanced band) then they would come to expect to be positioned by the band director where they will be most beneficial to the total group (team) performance, just as a coach positions the players on his team.

SCHEDULING CLASS LESSONS

A lesson time that is stable is the best, since the children can expect that they will go to their lesson at a certain time on a certain day. This can and does cause problems in the elementary school because in most cases a specific time is not alloted in the schedule for this type of instruction. Thus, the children will of necessity have to come out of the classroom for the lesson and miss a certain amount of regular class work each week. If the lesson can be arranged so that they occur during subjects like spelling, general music, art, physical education, etc., not much harm will be done, except perhaps creating a little animosity between a special teacher and the band director.

If the program is of sufficient size, the children should be grouped according to their ability. This adds problems to the scheduling of classes. It is most ideal to re-evaluate the children's abilities periodically and re-shuffle the class members. This allows for students who are advancing at a more rapid rate to move up into more advanced classes. A system of this kind puts one more burden on the schedule.

A rotating lesson schedule instantly solves many of these problems. This method, outlines of which appear in Illustrations 2-1 and 2-2, allows the child to miss, in some cases, one specific class every ten weeks if the instrumental teacher is in a school for an entire day. If the teacher only visits the school for a half-day, then the rotation comes around to the same class every five weeks.

An additional solution can and is easily suggested. Start the first class before school and hold one after school. This allows for a broader rotation schedule. This allows for fewer missed classes over the period of a semester. This, at first thought, would be excellent but consider that it has taken music a long time (and the band in particular) to be recognized as a worthy experience to be allowed into the school schedule. The director who allows the other teachers to back him off the school day is allowing himself to be subjected to the other "courses." He is admitting that band is not that important. He is allowing an irreparable blow to be dealt to his band program. Band, true, is not as important as math, science, English, etc., but it is a legitimate course if taught on sound educational principles. If it is not a curricular subject, it certainly is not to be considered an extra-curricular one. It should be however, defined and designated as a co-curricular subject worthy of school day time.

EXPLANATION OF THE CHARTS

Illustration 2-1 shows a rotating schedule for a morning session. As will be noted, Group IV comes for their lesson on September 4, at 10:00; on September 11, at 10:30; on September 18, at 11:00; on September 24, at 9:00; etc.

This chart also shows what can be done if there is an out-

ILLUSTRATION 2-1

ROTATING LESSON SCHEDULE

	9/4	9/11	9/18	9/25	10/2
	10/9	10/16	10/23	10/30	11/6
	11/13	11/20	12/4	12/11	12/18
	1/8				
9:00	I	II	III	IV	V
9:30	V	I	II	III	IV
10:00	IV	V	I	II	III
10:30	III	IV	V	I	II
11:00	II	III	IV	V	I

GROUP I	GROUP II	GROUP III	GROUP IV	GROUP V
D. Annep	L. Bauer	T. Wright	R. Ameduri	N. A. Boccardo
C. Beno	K. Becker		J. DeRosa	P. DeLuca
T. Camesano	A. Freauff		D. Folstad	R. Ruscine
R. Poccia	J. Haydock		R. Hulser	B. Rutherford
B. Race	G. Morice		S. Laux	M. Martin
P. Vashio	M. Roach		C. Louis	

standing student who deserves a private lesson. Note on Illustration 2-1 that Group III contains but one name. Thus this person would be receiving a private lesson during the semester.

Illustration 2-2 shows a rotating schedule that encompasses the entire school day.

The time for a band rehearsal can also be worked into either of the schedules. It may be desirable however, to give the band a static rehearsal time. This can be done by leaving the 11:00 slot vacant, or whatever time the director finds most desirable. Thus for a morning schedule the groups would only rotate over four periods rather than five. On the other hand, Group III slot could be designated as the band rehearsal time.

It is even possible to work out the group numbers so that if a few pupils are having trouble with particular subjects they will miss that particular class only once a semester if the full day schedule is used. Observe that Groups VII through X in Illustration 2-2 will miss but one class during the semester.

ILLUSTRATION 2-2

ROTATING LESSON SCHEDULE

	9/14 11/13	9/11 11/20	9/18 12/4	9/24 12/11	10/2 12/18	10/9 1/8	10/16	10/23	10/30	11/6
9:00	I	II	III	IV	V	VI	VII	VIII	IX	X
9:30	X	I	II	III	IV	V	VI	VII	VIII	IX
10:00	IX	X	I	II	III	IV	V	VI	VII	VIII
10:30	VIII	IX	X	I	II	III	IV	V	VI	VII
11:00	VII	VIII	IX	X	I	II	III	IV	V	VI
1:00	VI	VII	VIII	IX	X	I	II	III	IV	V
1:30	V	VI	VII	VIII	IX	X	I	II	III	IV
2:00	IV	V	VI	VII	VIII	IX	X	I	II	III
2:30	III	IV	V	VI	VII	VIII	IX	X	I	II
3:00	II	III	IV	V	VI	VII	VIII	IX	X	I

NOTE: The students in the various groups would be listed here

Though at the outset of this type of scheduling there will be the "forgetters," once it is established it runs along very smoothly. The entire schedule should be mimeographed and given to each child involved and one copy posted in a central location. Each date should be crossed off as it is passed so as to cut down on confusion. Students will learn to consult the chart each morning they have their lessons.

PRIVATE LESSONS

Some provision should be made for the outstanding child who will not only be bored but also discouraged by having to go over and over the same materials that the class is playing. The rotating schedule does allow for this but is hard to justify. Care must be taken here, however, so that parents do not think that their child, because he is not being given private lessons on school time, is being cheated. Many schools solve this by recommending outstanding students to study privately with persons outside of the school. Some school systems allow their teachers to use the schools in the evenings and on Saturdays to give these private lessons. If this practice is used, the parents are expected to pay a fee for these lessons. The band director should not be expected to spend additional hours outside of school time teaching lessons of this type without some sort of remuneration. This situation, however, usually occurs only after the children have had a semester or two or three of class lessons.

CURRICULUM

A carefully planned curriculum is the foundation upon which the instrumental program should rest. The strength or weakness of it determines to a great extent the success of the entire program. The curriculum content must be so constructed to include—first and most obviously, a logical and continued growth of the students' technical abilities on their respective instruments. This might be likened to the foundation of a house—and *only* the foundation. The complete house must have a frame. This frame is made up of the knowledge of the technical terminology upon which music is built. To have a sturdy frame the children must understand the hundreds of terms that are the language of music and be able to activate this language on their instruments. This knowledge is just as important to the musician as is the knowledge of where the second baseman is supposed to stand or what must be done when activating a center-line drive on a football team.

Too often, persons go all the way through grade school and high school band programs and come out being musically illiterate. All they can do is wiggle their fingers for certain tunes. They may have played the *Finale* to the *New World Symphony* but they could not sing the melody; would not know that there are any other parts and might not even recognize it if they were accidentally to hear it on the radio or T.V. Without some background explanation the intent of the composition could be completely misunderstood and go unrecognized.

The inside of this musical house contains many rooms—one for choir music; one for orchestra music; one for dramatic music like opera, oratorio, contata and ballet; one for solos; one for ensembles; and the one we are most interested in—the band! However, we must constantly keep an eye on small ensembles and solos for this is perhaps the best route through the house to the band room. The décor of the rooms contains examples of Renaissance, Baroque, Classical, Romantic and Contemporary just as each room in a house has electric lights, doors, windows and furniture.

A great number of children who pass through the bands will unfortunately lay aside their instruments after graduation. If their sojourn through the band program is to be of any lasting value, they must learn what "music" really is. Perhaps if the music teachers had been doing their jobs in the past, so as to be granted something like a AAA-1 rating in Dun & Bradstreet, the trash that the local disc jockeys call "music" would not stand a chance against the music of the real musical giants of the ages.

SYSTEMATIC APPROACH

A thoroughly systematic and methodical approach is necessary for any endeavor whether building a house, researching to find out how to invent the electric light, even going on a long trip, or teaching a child to play a musical instrument.

Most method books being published are so constructed that after the initial steps an outline is not absolutely necessary. By carefully selecting the succession of books, most items will be automatically taken care of by the book. But, notice the statement "*most* items will be taken care of by the book." Even with a good succession of exercise books it is still necessary to keep some record of what has been accomplished and what is to be accomplished. There are several ways in which this can be done.

One of the most obvious ways is by designing a curriculum outline. This type of outline is general, and as far as the teacher is concerned only a general one indeed. It merely gives the teacher or teachers in one school system a well defined *guide*— but only a guide. This type of outline does not completely cover all the various minor aspects of instrument instruction—all the fine points which actually spell the ultimate success.

A method that is used to assure uniformity of instruction in certain subjects throughout a school system is the establishment of uniform tests and examinations. The entire school system of New York State has a large number of state designed Regents Examinations. This can be done without too much difficulty in instrumental music on the local level. There is a danger, as happens in many cases in New York State, that some teachers end up teaching the *examination* instead of teaching the subject!

An inexperienced teacher could arbitrarily set up a test that might prove to be of too great a difficulty for each year of instruction. To avoid this problem he should keep accurate records of students' accomplishments over a period of time and then set up requirements based upon the records.

Not only are testing procedures of value in guiding the teacher along the correct path, and establishing a definite standard of giving marks for instrumental participation, but they can be an aid in upgrading the overall musical standard. Perhaps when the testing is first established in a new program it is established around the students' present abilities. As the program improves and teacher efficiency and effectiveness improves it is possible to increase the difficulty of the testing and accurately guide and increase the standard of the school's performance caliber.

A detailed outline is by far the best device for assuring an accurate, completely systematic approach. One can start an outline by merely following the materials included in the method book used for various learning levels. As one begins working out such an outline it will be found that certain items in method books need clarification. This will happen when one realizes, for example, that the flute players will have difficulty playing third space *C-sharp*. Perhaps they almost drop their flutes when playing the *D major* scale. This problem could have been solved beforehand had the teacher followed an outline that carefully taught the five contact points necessary when holding the flute. An outline for the clarinet *must* contain some work of going over the break before it is encountered in a piece of band music. Trombonists need some very careful explanations about the method of slurring while moving the slide so they do not get a glissando between notes. Brass players should not clean out their horns the night before a concert. All these things and the myriad of others are taken care of by a carefully constructed outline.

As for the various technical items necessary for an advanced player, the careful selection of instruction books will aid this. There are many sources for finding and selecting a logical progression of materials by merely consulting the various trade magazines like *The Instrumentalist*. Most texts designed for teaching teachers like the *Art of Saxophone Playing* by Larry Teal, published by Summy-Birchard, carry lists materials.

The Schmitt, Hall and McCreary Company publishes a series of booklets designed by Gerald Prescott that gives an outline of a systematic approach to certain exercise books for a careful development of technic. These outlines, entitled *The Prescott Technic System,* are published for the major instruments of the band including keyboard percussion. A complete discription of this system is given in *Getting Results with School Bands,* a book written by Gerald Prescott and Lawrence Chidester and published by Schmitt, Hall and McCreary.

On the following pages there, is an outline for teaching beginners the clarinet. The outline is meant merely as an example of the kind of care and detail that must be gone into *before* the children begin working out of an instruction book.

Notice items number one and nine at the beginning of the outline. It is important that the children take down in writing many items in the outline, such as the embouchure formation, parts of the instrument, assembling the instrument, etc. In their excitement to begin playing the instrument it is unlikely they will remember from one lesson to the next many items discussed. To facilitate matters the teacher may wish to mimeograph some items of information. In this case it would be better for the children to have a loose-leaf notebook in which to keep this information.

OUTLINE FOR TEACHING THE CLARINET TO BEGINNERS

I. Preliminaries

A. *Equipment Needed by Students*
   1. spiral notebook for notes and assignments
   2. folding music stand
   3. music carrying case
   4. chamois clarinet swab
   5. cork grease
      place and sit quietly.
   6. reed guard

7. four clarinet reeds
8. package of pipe cleaners
9. pencil and pen
10. dish towel for first lessons

B. *A Dozen Don'ts!*
1. Don't toot when you are not supposed to.
2. Don't toot on the playground or in the halls or any place that may cause a disturbance to others.
3. Don't talk out in class unless you raise your hand first. Sit quietly until recognized. Don't wave your hand in the air while waiting, just hold it still.
4. Don't constantly look out the windows, at the bulletin board, at other persons, at other books and objects or peer into the hall everytime someone walks past. Keep full attention directed toward the teacher and to what is being taught.
5. Don't use the instrument as a hammer, battle ax, or other defensive weapon.
6. Don't use the instrument as a football, basketball, baseball bat or other piece of sports equipment.
7. Don't allow others to blow your instrument.
8. Don't open the case on the playground or other places where damage might be inflicted accidentally.
9. Don't store the instrument at home in such a place where others might open the case and play with it. Keep it in a special storage place out of the reach of smaller brothers and sisters and out of sight of older people.
10. Don't let it get dirty. Clean it out regularly.
11. Don't forget your instrument on lesson day.
12. Don't forget your book on lesson day and keep it clean by carrying it to school in a carrying case.

C. *Class Procedures*
1. Enter the lesson room at least two minutes before the class is to start.
2. If a class is still in the room, stand or sit in a place to facilitate their exit.
3. As soon as they have vacated the premises, take your
4. Sit quietly with your instrument in its case. Just open

the lesson book to the assigned page and look it over one final time. Note what things you had difficulty with and how to solve the problems that might arise.

5. Instruments may be removed from the cases only upon the teacher's signal. The cases must be opened in as quiet a fashion as possible. Do not let the catches snap open. This merely contributes to a noisy, undisciplined class.

6. Place the instrument case under the chair or in a place out of the teacher's path.

7. Place the instrument in rest position and await instructions.

At the conclusion of class:

8. The lesson is concluded when the teacher dismisses the class.

9. Be sure to clean out the instrument before it is placed in the case.

10. If the instrument is not to be taken back to the classroom, place it in its appropriate storage place out of traffic lanes.

D. *Basic Parts of the Clarinet*
1. mouthpiece with cap, ligature and reed
2. barrel
3. lower section—the largest and longest piece
4. next longest piece is the upper section
5. bell

E. *The Reed*
1. The reed is made from a type of grass cane known as Arundo donax that grows on the border of the Mediterranean Sea in southern France, cut and aged for two years.
2. The parts of the reed:
   a. tip—the very thin fragile edge that vibrates. At no time should anything be allowed to come in contact with the edge. The slightest nick may cause difficulties in blowing.
   b. vamp—the cut part
   c. stock—the uncut area
   d. butt—the blunt, thick end

F. *The Mouthpiece*
  1. It is the most important part of the clarinet. A poor mouthpiece is the greatest deterent to good playing.
  2. Parts of the mouthpiece:
     a. table—the flat surface on which the reed rests
     b. lay or facing—the area under the vibrating portion of the reed
     c. throat—the part below the long hole or mouthpiece window
     d. bore—the rounded interior
     e. cork tenon

II. First Steps to Playing

A. *Assembling the Reed on the Mouthpiece*
  1. Take everything off the mouthpiece
  2. Place the vamp of the reed into the mouth about a half minute or until the tip is flat.
     a. When water is absorbed into the reed, it becomes less brittle and allows the reed to vibrate
     b. If the tip wrinkles it can be pressed on something flat and held there momentarily. This usually helps flatten out the tip area.
  3. Place the ligature over the mouthpiece so that the screws are above the table.
     a. The ligature should be placed so it is just below the ligature guide lines or in such a position that it will be on the stock of the reed.
  4. Place the flat surface of the reed on the table of the mouthpiece and pass the butt end under the ligature.
     a. Keep the fingers away from the tip!
  5. Line the thin edge of the reed with the edge of the mouthpiece.
     a. Do not allow anything to come in contact with the edge—line it up merely by sight
     b. If the reed is too high, the clarinet will blow hard.
     c. If the reed is too low, the clarinet will blow too easily or not blow at all.
  6. When the reed is properly in line, and the ligature is

below the mark, tighten the screws only slightly.

a. Tighten the ligature just enough to hold the reed in place.

b. If the screws are too tight, they will stop the reed from vibrating freely. If the ligature is left tight the pressure may warp the mouthpiece.

THINGS TO REMEMBER:

1. If wrinkles do not straighten out after wetting the reed in the mouth for a few minutes, they can be removed by pressing the tip on a flat surface and holding it down for a few seconds.
2. When the reed becomes chipped or cracked, throw it away and use a new one.
3. If the vamp becomes dirty, wash it with a little soap or replace it. This will not happen if you make sure your hands are clean before playing the clarinet.
4. Do not store dirty or cracked reeds in the case. Throw them away!
5. Dirty reeds can lead to lip sores and mouth infections. The reed only costs about 35¢ but a doctor bill will be considerably more.

Embouchure—the formation of the lips and facial muscles around the mouthpiece

1. Place the lower lip slightly over the lower teeth.
   a. One-half of the red portion covers the teeth
2. Set the reed on the lower lip
   a. About one-half inch from the end of the reed— thumb-nail distance
3. Set the upper teeth on the mouthpiece about one-half inch from the tip.
4. Close the upper lip around the mouthpiece
   a. Do not move the lower lip
   b. Corners of the lips must be firm against the teeth and in a slight smile
5. Stretch or point the chin so that it is in a position of pulling down
   a. It must never be bunched up under the reed

6. The angle of the mouthpiece should be about 40 degrees

NOTE: Sucking hard on a soda straw will give the basic embouchure formation for all instruments—chin down, corners of the mouth firm.

III *Playing Procedure*

A. *First Steps*
1. The mouthpiece is placed into the barrel
2. Form the embouchure step by step
3. Press the lower lip against the reed just enough to exert pressure against the reed
    a. Do not bite the mouthpiece with both sets of teeth
    b. Demonstrate a ruler vibrating on a hard surface and on a soft surface—hard surface sounds good, soft—practically no sound at all. The lower lip if firm and the chin is pulled down is like a very hard surface
4. The tone is started by whispering "who"
    a. No attempt must be made at tonguing at this point
5. Blow firmly into the mouthpiece like blowing out 25 candles on a cake, keeping a slight smile and smooth chin.
    a. Practice by blowing air at the palm of the hand held six inches in front of the mouth and also by sizzling to give the idea of air pressure
6. The tongue is to rest on the bottom of the mouth

TROUBLES IN BLOWING?

1. A bubbling sound—remove the saliva from behind the reed
2. No tone—you are gripping the reed too firmly and not letting it vibrate
3. If air rushes through but there is no tone:
    a. Not supporting the reed with the lip
    b. The reed may not be on the mouthpiece properly
    c. The reed may be too hard, try another one

4. The mouthpiece may not be far enough into the mouth
5. A high pitched squeak—too much of the mouthpiece is in the mouth or you are blowing too hard
6. A very thin, wavering tone
   a. The smile in the embouchure has been lost—lips are allowed to become flabby and come away from the teeth
   b. The mouthpiece is not far enough in the mouth
   c. There is not enough pressure from the lower lip against the reed
      (1) Hold the barrel with the right hand and press the left hand on top. If the tone immediately gets higher the pressure was not great enough from the lower lip

NOTE: The pitch produced using the correct pressure usually will be between *F* and *G* on the piano

7. If the tone produced is flat in pitch try:
   a. A little more grip on the embouchure
   b. Adding to the speed of the air
   c. Taking a little more mouthpiece into the mouth

IV. *Practice Procedure*

A. Practice on the mouthpiece and barrel only—It might be wise for the children to leave their instruments in school. The dish towel suggested under "Equipment needed by students" would be used for the children to take home just the mouthpiece and barrel. A large rubber band would hold it together.
1. Practice holding the tone steady for as long as possible
   a. Time it with a second hand of a clock
   b. Keep track of the time and try to make it five seconds longer each day
2. Hold the tone for four beats with four beats rest between
   a. Do this eight times
3. Hold the tone for six beats with four beats rest between
   a. Do this about eight times

4. Hold the tone for eight beats with four beats rest between
   a. Do this about eight times

REMEMBER:

1. Practice in front of a mirror, checking each stage of the embouchure each time you begin.
2. Each time you play, remove the reed and soak it in the mouth.
3. When finished playing, dry off the reed and place it on the reed guard and place the mouthpiece cap over the ligature and mouthpiece. Roll the pieces in the dish towel.
4. Practice only the time designated and no longer. The lip muscles will tire and forcing them will do more harm than good.
5. The first objective in playing any instrument is to be able to produce a pleasing tone. This is most easily accomplished by playing with the proper embouchure, listening to the tone, and making whatever corrections may be necessary.

V. *Add these parts to the list under I-D*

1. tenon receivers and tenon rings
2. bridge key
3. keys
4. springs—needle and flat
5. rods
6. pivot and hinge screws
7. tone holes
8. tone hole rings
9. pads
10. key spatula
11. pad seats
12. cork tenon
13. thumb rest

VI. *Assembling the Clarinet*

A.   Place the case on a flat, level surface—do not hold it on the lap!
1. Place the reed in the mouth
2. Apply cork grease to each corn tenon if needed
     a. As each piece is greased, place it back in the case
     b. If a lot of grease accumulates on the parts, wipe it off with a cloth
     c. Only a litle grease should be applied
3. Lift the lower end of the lower joint with the first finger of the right hand so the left hand can slide under
     a. With the left palm up, pick up the lower joint under the bottom where there are no keys
4. Pick up the bell in the right hand
5. Slide the lower joint into the bell—turning as they are pushed together
6. Hold the lower section in the right hand
     a. The thumb and first finger around the lower section
     b. Fingers must not be placed over the lower rods
7. Pick up the upper section in the right hand
     a. With the palm down, rotate the section on its top in the case until the fingers overlap the two rings
     b. Turn the palm up so that the section is the reverse of the way it was in the case and the rings, covered by the fingers are now up
     c. Slide the upper section into the lower, turning as they are pushed together
     d. Line up the bridge keys
          (1) When turning the sections together, be sure the bridge keys do not hit together but that the bridge key of the upper section slides over that of the lower section. This is done by making sure the fingers cover the rings of the upper section.
8. Place the barrel on while resting the bell on a chair or table

      a. The right hand holds the top part of the upper joint turning as they are pushed together

9. Place the mouthpiece into the barrel
   a. Line the hole of the mouthpiece with the thumb rest and the G hole on the back of the clarinet
10. With the bell still on the table, place the reed on the mouthpiece

VII. Disassembling the Clarinet

1. Remove the reed and place it on the reed guard
2. Remove the mouthpiece by turning it slightly as it is pulled out of the barrel's tenon receiver
   a. Place the mouthpiece cover over the mouthpiece and ligature and place it in its appropriate well in the case
3. Slide the weighted end of the swab through the instrument—bell first
   a. Do not drop it down as it might damage the bore or dent the vent keys that project into the bore
   b. Make sure the swab is not bunched up
   c. Pull the swab slowly through the bore to collect all the moisture
4. Remove the barrel next and proceed down the instrument
   a. As each part is dismantled, lay it in its well in the case
   b. If moisture has collected in the tenon receivers, wipe it out with the swab

VIII. First Tones

A. *Partial Position*
1. The thumb rest is held betwen the thumb and first finger of the right hand. The thumb on top, the thumb rest resting on the second joint of the first finger
2. The left hand is held around the barrel
3. The instrument is held at about 40 degrees from the body

4. Head up; good posture

B. *Blowing*

   1. Practice as in IV, Numbers A-1 through 4

      a. This note is *G* and appears on the second line of the staff

         (1) Memorize: No fingers down—the note is *G*—appears on the second line of the staff

C. Place the left thumb over the single hole on the back of the clarinet

   1. The thumb must touch the hole on the cushiony part and lay at a nearly perpendicular angle to the instrument. It must not be parallel to the instrument!

   2. Practice as in IV, Numbers A-1 through 4

      a. This note is *F* and is in the first space of the staff

         (1) Memorize: Thumb down—the note is *F*—appears in the first space of the staff

D. Leaving the thumb in place, place the first finger on the uppermost of the six holes

   1. Proceed as above

E. As above using the note *D*

F. As above using the note middle *C*

   1. The children should become familiar with the term "middle *C*" and why it is called "middle *C*"

IX. *Home Practice Procedures*

A. Practice thirty minutes each day broken into three segments of ten minutes each

   1. First practice session:

      a. Practice as in IV, Numbers A-1 through 4

   2. Second practice session:

      a. Practice as in VIII

   3. Third practice session:

      a. Practice as in IV, Numbers A-1 through 4 but use the notes *G, F, E, D,* and *C,* moving up and down after each rest, i.e., *G*—rest—*F*—rest—*E*—rest, etc.

X. *Articulation*

A. *Basic Knowledge*

1. Four quarter notes are merely one whole note interrupted three times
   a. The momentary stop of the sound is created by the tongue touching the reed and stopping it from vibrating
      (1) There is *NO* stoppage of the flow of air during the course of four consecutive quarter notes
      (2) The tip of the tongue touches the tip of the reed—not tip to tip but overlapping each other ever so slightly
      (3) The tongue must move only at the front section, like saying "tu," "du," or "te." The vowel sound must be nasal in quality so the sound is placed high and toward the front of the mouth, not a gutteral sound that might be created when saying "gah" as in "gotten" or a flattened tongue in "tah" as in "top"
2. *Methods of Stopping the Tone*
   a. With the breath
   b. With the tongue
   c. By removing the instrument from the mouth
   d. By closing the embouchure—thus shutting off the air with the lip pressure on the reed
   e. By stopping the flow of air at the throat like saying "rug" or "tug"
      (1) Methods "a" and "b" are the only correct ways. All the others must not be allowed to be used
3. Method "a" is the normal method of stopping a tone and to be used at the early stages of playing
4. Method "b" is used in staccato playing but ONLY with advanced players

B. *Step-by-Step Procedures for Consecutive Notes*
1. Without the instrument
   a. Sing "whooodooodooodooo" noting the action of the tongue and breath
      (1) The breath flows constantly for the four beats
      (2) The tongue merely interrupts the sound momentarily when it touches the top of the mouth
      (3) There is no motion except the front part of the tongue

(a) Children could close their eyes so they can concentrate on the action of the tongue

2. With the instrument (with mouthpiece and barrel only)

   a. Instead of the tongue touching the roof of the mouth, it will contact the front tip of the reed

   b. Teacher holds lower arm parallel with the floor with the hand in a relaxed position position hanging downward

      (1) The hand represents the front portion of the tongue

      (2) Start a tone with "whooo"

      (3) When the teacher raises the hand, the children raise the tongue in the mouth and let it flop down instantly after the contact is made

   d. The teacher moves the hand up and down at varying intervals of time so the children do not know when the motion will occur.

      (1) The resulting sound would appear like: "whoooooooooodoooooodooooooooooodoodooooo" etc.

      (a) Do this several times

3. Do this above procedure on the instruments with various pitches

4. On a single note play a whole note, a whole rest, four quarter notes, whole rest, whole note, whole rest, four quarter notes, etc.

   a. Be sure the sound being created in the third measure is one of perfect legato

   b. Be sure that there is no outward motion, i.e., a motion of the chin, jaw or neck muscles

   c. Remember—the air must flow constantly during the quarter notes just as it does during the course of the whole note—the tongue merely interrupts the reed's vibrations three times

5. The secret to good articulation lies in maintaining a constant flow of air during the course of several notes that are to be articulated

      a. A check can be made on the air flow by allowing air to escape around the sides of the mouthpiece. This means a child will have to relax the embouchure. This does change the embouchure slightly but aids in checking this important concept

C. *Starting the Tone with the Tongue*

  1. Place the tongue on the reed

  2. Blow

      a. A small amount of air pressure is to be built up behind the tongue

  3. Allow the tongue to flop away from the reed

      a. Do not force additional air into the mouth as the tongue moves away from the reed

         (1) The tongue should merely move away from the reed and allow it to begin vibrating

            (a) Too much air pressure will result in an accented attack

            (b) Too little air pressure will result in a fuzzy beginning of the tone

               ((1)) Experimentation on the part of the student must be done till they determine the exact amount of pressure that is needed before releasing the reed

  4. Stop the tone by making a sound like "tah"

      a. The air merely stops flowing from out of the lungs

      b. If difficulty in stopping occurs like the appearance of a "tutting" sound or a "dug," breathe in through the mouth at the instant the note is to be stopped or say "tar"

         (1) Only after many months of instruction should the children be taught to stop the tone with the tongue

3

Teaching Specific Exercises in the Elementary Band

Illustration 3-1 shows what might be found in a typical band method that uses the whole note instructional system. It does not suffice, when starting a beginning instrumental class, to merely put an instrument in the child's hands, open the book to the first lesson and proceed to play. A great deal of pre-book instruction must preceed this first musical exercise. This instruction must include information like that found in the previous chapter along with the students having a thorough knowledge of the counting of rhythm, reading the letter names of the notes and understanding such terminology as the meaning of the meter signature, G clef, value of whole notes and whole rests, how the position of the note relates to pitch and fingering of the instrument, etc.

It is extremely important to the success of a band program to have the children understand how to keep track of rhythm while they are playing their instruments. This author is a very strong advocate of the tapping of the foot. (The reader is referred to an article by this author on that subject entitled "Toward More Accurate Rhythm" in the September 1968 issue of *The Instrumentalist.*) The necessity for a knowledge of all these things before the first exercise can be played properly gives valid reasons and makes for a strong recommendation for the establishment of a pre-band program. The pre-band program effectively teaches all these fundamentals long before the children have to encounter the difficulty of a complicated band instrument with all its embouchure, finger and lip coordination problems.

ILLUSTRATION 3-1

It has been said many, many times that the teacher must have a specific purpose or aim in mind for each exercise and that the children should know just what this aim or purpose is. The aim or purpose for this, the first written exercise, providing the aforementioned groundwork has been laid, would be to get the children acquainted with reading notes and their relation to the blowing and fingering technic on the instrument while maintaining good posture, proper embouchure and hand positions.

PROCEDURES FOR PLAYING THE FIRST EXERCISE — ILLUSTRATION 3-1

The procedure for playing all exercises for several weeks is as follows:

First—set the fingers—check the position of the hands
Second—set the embouchure
Third—start the foot (up—now—down-up-down-up-etc.)
Fourth—play. . . . .

Now a question as to perfection should be answered. The degree of perfection that should be achieved is determined through a decision as to the aims one wishes to achieve before proceeding on the next exercise. Of course, the total aims do not have to be achieved with the first or second playing but the children should be totally aware what those aims are. Again, a notebook may be of help so the children can write down what the aims are. And, why shouldn't the teacher expect that for the next lesson the children could, with a sheet of blank paper, write out what the aims for the week's lesson were?

There are a few "errors" that the teacher may allow to creep into the class's playing at this first attempt but which ultimately must be corrected—within a week in any event. The teacher need not confuse the children at this point with their holding the note out for four full counts. If the teacher's system is such that the use of the tongue is not yet introduced, the ictus of each child's tone might not be at the exact rhythmic spot.

The aims that must be achieved are:

1. Achieve proper embouchure while playing
2. Maintain proper finger and hand position
3. Activate the foot so it presents a steady flow of the beats

There will no doubt be a problem of individual intonation at this point. If there is some especially faulty intonation the teacher will probably be able to straighten it out by merely observing the various embouchures. As the teacher walks around the class between the rows, he can say "check that embouchure," "pull the chin down" or "point that chin!" A little adjustment of the tuning mechanism of an individual's instrument may be necessary, but if their breathing and embouchure is correct, little more should have to be said at this point.

If there is an embouchure problem, it merely means that a firm foundation has not been established. Any further progress will be slow and infuse this faulty embouchure deeper into the child's technic. This is where the lesson is a gigantic problem. What does a teacher do if five members of the class are playing with good embouchures but one is not? Should the class continue without the book? If this is done the teacher may loose the interest of those who have already achieved good embouchers. But, if the teacher continues forward, this one student may no doubt be lost. If there are two or even three poor embouchures it may be worth the teacher's and class's time to back up and continue to do remedial work on this embouchure.

There are two solutions to this problem. The first is for the teacher to call the student in at a separate time and work separately with him. This may have to be done before or after school. More practice on the part of the child may be of no avail, especially if the teacher is certain the child has been trying. Additionally, the teacher could assign one of the children in class who does have a good embouchure to aid this student. He could also contact the parent and instruct him in what has to be done and what should be achieved. A note to the parent may do some good, but a personal telephone call or a visit to the home and a few minutes of a lesson in front of the parent will pay large dividends. The parent may be invited to school, at which time the child, teacher and parent discuss the problem. These last few suggestions take considerable time and may not be possible or even desirable. Shouldn't the child be responsible for these things himself? Should the teacher coddle each child? Or, is the teacher just conscious about the success of the children in his classes?

A point that should not pass our observation here is that if the program of adaptation classes was successful, this problem should not have arisen in the first place. Or, if the pre-book instruction was successful, this problem should have been solved earlier. It is almost too late.

The tone quality is also to be observed, but if the breath and embouchure is being activated correctly, the quality should be fairly good. This fundamental also rests on the pre-book instruction work and how well the foundations have been laid.

If the exercise is not played perfectly the first time (i.e., someone does not count, does not keep the foot going, makes a squeak [in the case of the single reeds] or the wrong pitch [in the case of the brass] or players play too few or too many notes) the exercise should be repeated. These problems usually do not arise if there has been a pre-band program.

At a second playing, the children should be given further instructions on what to do or how to improve the rendition. Stating some of the many popular bromides will be of some help here—"Be sure you blow through the instrument," hold the embouchure firm throughout the four beats." Better yet, give them a new technic to use like: "This time during the rest think: check—hands—embouchure—breath." The teacher should say these four words aloud during the next rendering of the exercise.

Should the children "play" the eight measures? Is it just a rest at the end? Certainly the rest should be "played." To be able to render this exercise with complete perfection, everything written on the score must be observed. If the children do not have to observe this, the teacher is effectively teaching them *not* to observe everything. If in the very first reading lesson the teacher allows the children to disregard something, no matter how minor one way may think it to be, then the teacher is teaching them to play incorrectly. Later, if the child is allowed to disregard this whole measure of four beats, he will find himself disregarding such things as accents, dynamics—after all, these are not really so important either.

Two more items have to be observed—the starting and stopping of the whole note. Do all the members of the class begin the tone precisely, together with a good attack—making proper use of the tongue, and do they stop the tone at the end of the fourth beat at the same time in the same manner?

It may be well to review the action of the tongue when starting the tone (Chapter 2—Outline for Teaching the Clarinet to Beginners) and the means of stopping the tone. Accuracy in ending the whole note together will be aided by a brief discussion of the concept that is somewhat unusual when first considered. . . . This concept may be graphically shown by drawing Illustrations 3-2 and 3-3 on the chalk board.

ILLUSTRATION 3-2

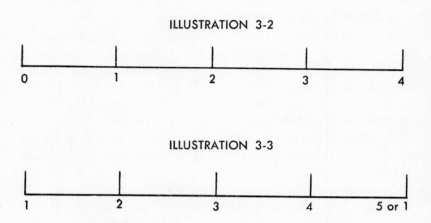

ILLUSTRATION 3-3

Illustration 3-2 is a ruler. With a ruler we have the first inch and then call it number "1". We have the second inch and call it number "2" etc. But in music we say "one" then play the tone. We say "two" then play the tone as in Illustration 3-3. So, if one were to count: "one, two, three, four" and stop, it would be like cutting off the fourth beat about a quarter of a beat past the fourth beat. What has been played then is in reality a dotted half note tied to an eighth or sixteenth, not a full whole note. Stopping at count four would be like executing the whole note as shown in Illustration 3-4.

If one were going to play a full whole note he must not stop the tone until the instant the fifth beat (or the first beat of the next measure) were to begin (see Illustration 3-5) .

ILLUSTRATION 3-4

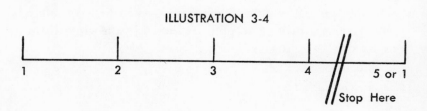

ILLUSTRATION 3-5

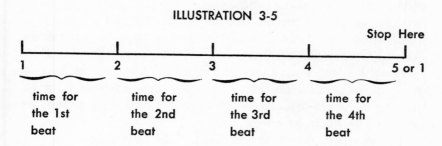

In reality, in order to play a half note the count must be three —not three beats, but the end is at "three" not after "two." This concept will aid in playing quarter notes that are followed by quarter rests. If the children understand that a note has to have length, part of the problem of "tutting" may be solved before it is acquired.

Illustration 3-6 shows an exposure to motor (finger) responses on the part of the woodwind instruments and lip movements for the brass.

Added to the responses necessary for Illustration 3-1, Illustration 3-6 calls for the clarinets to lift four fingers—more accurately, three fingers and the thumb. The aim would be to have the woodwinds move their fingers quickly, as soon as the first note has concluded. Do not allow the class members to wait until the fourth beat of the second measure (the rest) to move. The teacher here can exercise the practice of positive approach by first stating the exercise's aim: i.e., the moving of the fingers quickly upon the conclusion of the note. Do not wait until the class has played the exercise and then tell them what they should have done.

ILLUSTRATION 3-6

If the pre-book instruction period has laid groundwork in finger movement there should be no trouble. If some trouble is experienced some silent practice will be in order. Silent practice will be of particular aid for the flutes and alto saxophones. (This is, assuming the notes of Illustration 3-6 are written notes for the clarinets and cornets.)

For the silent practicing, clarinetists should rest the bell of their instruments upon their knee; the flutes, the foot joint on the knee; and the saxophones, rest the bell of the instrument on the chair between the knees.

The students should be reminded of the following finger motion rules:

1. Move the fingers to the position of the following note the instant the note presently being played has concluded.
2. Move all necessary fingers simultaneously.
3. The fingers not in use (covering tone holes or activating keys) are to remain close to their respective tone holes or keys.

The silent practice may be aided by having one student play his instrument while the rest of the class merely finger. (Do not forget to start by getting the foot moving first.) Those not playing would say:

on the first beat of the whole note: "blow"
on the second beat of the whole note: "check"
on the third beat of the whole note: "fingers"
on the fourth beat of the whole note: "and"
on the first beat of the rest: "move" (to the next note)
on the second beat of the rest: "check"
on the third beat of the rest: "fingers"
on the fourth beat of the rest: "breath and"
on the first beat of the whole note: "blow"
etc.

For the flutes and alto saxophones the children should be told exactly which fingers are to be moved between the first and second note.

Assuming the clarinet and cornet notes are those written, the flutes would be playing third line B-flat to fifth line F. This is one of the good arguments for not starting heterogeneous classes because the flutes must move thusly:

first finger of the left hand—up
second finger of the left hand—down
third finger of the left hand—down
first finger of the right hand—down
second finger of the right hand—down

The brass have a whole different group of problems facing them in Illustration 3-6. Perhaps in an effort to be positive we should not say "problems" but "a whole different group of challenges."

These "challenges" of course will not be new or problems at all if the pre-book instruction period has been successful.

The exercise in Illustration 3-7 entails the use of:

1. Legato articulation
2. Breathe between consecutively articulated notes
3. Moving fingers during the momentary pause between consecutively articulated notes.

ILLUSTRATION 3-7

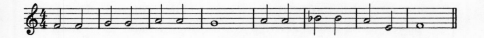

Step number 1 in the positive approach would be to sing the rhythm with Illustration 3-8 written on the chalk board. Point out the commas over the third, fifth and seventh bars. Tell the class that the comma means they are to breathe at these three points. Inform the class that the first bar is the one that appears *before* the G clef. (This last explanation is necessary so that terminology in regards to counting bars will be clear to the class.)

ILLUSTRATION 3-8

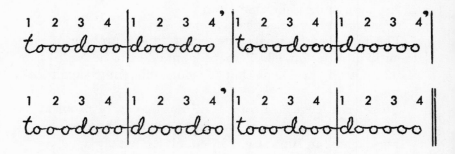

Have the children notice the lines connecting all the letters except at the end of the second, fourth, and sixth measures. Notice also that in these measures there appears to be one "o" missing at the end of the measure—under the comma. Though we talked earlier about playing the whole note for four *full* beats, it is now necessary to abbreviate this note in order to re-store some air to the lungs before continuing. The children therefore should know that in this case it is legal to play the measures differently than written. The half note is actually played like a quarter with a dot followed by an eighth rest. The whole note is played like a half note tied to a dotted quarter followed by an eighth rest. The class should be told: "composers, when writing a piece, know this will be done at times. The reason it is not written like it is played is merely because it is easier to write one half note rather than a quarter note, a dot and a rest. Likewise, it is easier to write one whole note rather than a half note tied to a dotted-quarter and an eighth rest. It may also be the desire of a performer not to observe the breath marks as they are written. A written-in rest would des-troy what could be a different interpretation of this piece. We will play this piece with some different interpretations so you will see exactly what can be done with a simple line of music."

NOTE: the last measure does have this last "o". This whole note DOES get four *full* beats.

Step number 2 will be the playing of the exercise on a single pitch so as to concentrate on the motion of the tongue. It is also advisable to play the first two measures being sure the breath is taken at the correct time. The necessity for checking the exact point at which the breath is taken is so sufficient time is given so the next note may be articulated at the proper time, i.e., at the instant the foot contacts the floor for that beat. If the breath is not taken soon enough, the children probably will not play the next note together.

Step number 3—play five notes taking the breath where the comma is.

Step number 4—have one or two individuals play to demonstrate to the class (and to the teacher). The class could even be asked to close their eyes to listen. When the demonstrator has played his five notes ask the children to raise their hands if they think it was performed correctly. Someone playing might get caught sleeping for some child might catch one not playing the fifth note correctly. It should be played with two full beats, not one-and-a-half like it was the end of a group before a breath mark.

After the exercise is played correctly in its entirety the teacher should show how this exercise can be interpreted differently. Illustrations 3-9 through 3-14 are some suggested interpretations. This might only be done after a week's practice or even two week's practice on the exercise.

These illustrations could be mimeographed and passed out to the class. This would facilitate teaching these variations and give the students something to refer to while the teacher is discussing and demonstrating.

Keeping in mind that all things should have a purpose, several ideas will be accomplished by doing the above. The first will be to show the children that there are different ways of playing a piece of music. This is introducing the idea of interpretation in music at a very early stage. It will also show the children that a bar line does not mean anything more than a

ILLUSTRATION 3-9—original

ILLUSTRATION 3-10—as the original would be played

ILLUSTRATION 3-11—first interpretative variation

ILLUSTRATION 3-12—as the first variation would be played

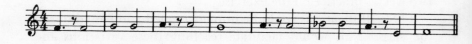

ILLUSTRATION 3-13—second interpretative variation

ILLUSTRATION 3-14—as the second variation would be played

definition in time. It will also show that the second bar does not necessarily mean a breath. This will be of special value for the flutes to see. It also shows that a whole note is not always the end of a phrase and that there are such things as "phrases," i.e., sentences within a line of music.

The exercise in Illustration 3-15 would be the type found in the first lesson of a fast moving beginning method. This would not be one of the first exercises but maybe the fourth or fifth. It would also appear in a book using the whole note approach but probably not until the third or fourth or in some cases the sixth or seventh lesson.

The technics to be learned in this exercise would include:
1. Articulating of reiterated quarter notes
2. The movement to another note within a group of reiterated notes
3. Proper methods of observing the quarter rests
   a. Sometimes a breath is allowable
   b. Sometimes a rest is only a rhythmic silence
4. Repeat sign

A brief review of the specific technics learned on the fore-going exercises are once again in order. The review is given

ILLUSTRATION 3-15

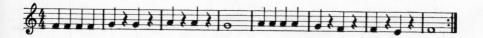

here not because the writer feels the reader may have forgotten the specific technics but to further enforce the idea that review and re-review is one of the secrets to learning.

The teacher may desire at this point to have the children list all the following points. A mimeographed sheet or copying them off the board into their notebooks would be in order. At the next lesson the teacher could prepare a little test or merely have the children write out the list from memory. This quiz would also include the material discussed for the exercise in Illustration 3-15.

Those technics acquired to this point include:

1. Maintainance of proper embouchure while playing and reading
2. Maintainance of proper finger and hand positions while playing
3. Activate the foot so it presents a steady flow of the rhythm
4. During the rests think: "check—hands—embouchure—breathe"
5. Observe everything and play everything on the score—even the whole rest at the end
6. Play the whole note for four full beats—do not stop the tone until the first beat of the succeeding measure begins
7. Move fingers simultaneously
8. Move the fingers the instant the tone of the note has ended —for brass players, make lip adjustments and mentally hear the next pitch as soon as the present note has ended
9. Woodwinds: the fingers not in use (covering tone holes or activating keys) are to remain close to their respective tone holes or keys
   Brass: keep fingers in contact with the valve buttons

An excellent way to test the childrens' real knowledge of those problems involved is to have one class member or the teacher play an exercise purposefully incorrect and have the children answer questions about the performance. Some of the things that could be done is to play with a poor embouchure, not hold the last note of a group of half notes for its full duration or take a breath at every rest.

This fourth exercise is loaded with pitfalls. These pitfalls can be avoided by the positive approach again, i.e., telling the children what has to be done.

The teacher should demonstrate the first five notes and point out:

1. The five notes are to be separated by legato articulation
2. Mentally, one should hear this as five consecutively connected notes being detached only by four flips of the tongue
3. The fifth note is to be ended with the stoppage of the breath
4. The embouchure, during the rest (2nd beat, 2nd measure) is to retain its position without relaxation.

The class or some members of the class should then be directed to play the first five notes, all on the same pitch. They should be directed to hold the embouchure without moving during the rest. Thus they will actually perform: 1-2-3-4-5-rest-relax.

It should be pointed out that a "rest" does not necessarily mean "relax." Most times a rest is merely a rhythmic silence— only sometimes does it mean "relax."

The tempo used for the first attempts should be slow (about

$\quad = 60)$. This will give the children and teacher a chance

to see that the "rest" is being treated properly followed by a relaxation at the proper rhythmic point.

The next step to be taken will be determined by the class itself and the interpretation the teacher uses in playing this exercise. If this is a flute class or large mouthpiece brass, the next step may be that shown in Illustration 3-16 with regard to taking of a breath. Especially in the case of the flutes, it is unlikely that by this time they will be able to play to the end of the fourth measure without taking a breath. If this is a heterogeneous class everyone will of necessity be instructed to

ILLUSTRATION 3-16

breathe in the same place at the outset. Later the breathing can be arranged to suit each group of individual instruments. If at all possible the clarinets, cornets and horns should breathe in places indicated in Illustration 3-17.

ILLUSTRATION 3-17

There is one other item that might be accomplished here. The breathing at the end of the fourth measure gives what might be a typical interpretation of this line. However, consider the interpretation given if the breath marks are placed as shown in Illustration 3-18.

The placement of the breath marks in Illustration 3-18 will do several things musically. First, it will mean that the whole note in measure four will be given its four full beats and lead to the line of quarter notes. It would also break down the "tyranny of the bar line." If the repeat is used, the last note would lead into the four quarter notes of the first measure. This in turn would tie these eight measures into a single unit that has musical direction.

One more item of interpretation could be utilized. Have the class carry the sound of the whole note over into the next quarters by making a slight crescendo.

ILLUSTRATION 3-18

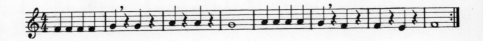

One can see that poor habits may inadvertently be acquired by beginners because of the teacher's lack of careful fore-thought. Take for example Illustration 3-15, written like it might be incorrectly played—as shown in Illustration 3-19. If care is not taken students may breathe at every bar line (particularly the flutes).

The fourth note in the first measure would be rendered like a sixteenth note. It would be found that if the taking of a breath is not carefully taught, the note before a breath may end up being very short indeed. This is more often than not tied to the problem of stopping the breath. If this most important point is overlooked in the teaching, this fourth note will end up with a "tut" or a "tug" or some other incorrect manner of stopping the sound. This then may very well be carried over into the second measure making those quarter notes very short also.

It may even be found that without careful instruction as to the difference between a "relaxing" rest and a rest that merely represents a rhythmic silence, the children will be relaxing during every rest. Tuba players are best known for this bad habit. Watch a tuba player during a march—he will invariably relax the embouchure after every note because he has quarter notes, quarter rests all the way through.

Unless time is taken to discuss and re-review the items covering the stopping of the breath, great problems in articulation will begin to be formed whenever the children practice an exercise that contains a note, a rest, a note, a rest, etc. The teacher may deem it necessary to also teach the children how to stop the tone with the tongue, i.e., without stopping the breath on the quarter notes. However, this technic might better be saved for more advanced work when speed is necessary. At the slow

ILLUSTRATION 3-19

speeds used by beginners, the breath release would be the best technic to use.

Tone and intonation may also be affected by lack of care in observing proper places at which to breathe. If great care is not taken to teach the children exactly when the whole note in the fourth measure ends (i.e., if a breath is to be used, on the "and" after "four") the children will have a tendency to merely let their air run out. They will thus be pretty well out of air so will let the breath line sage creating a flatting of the tone and diminishing its quality. Some will attempt to hold the pitch up by squeezing with the embouchure. This is when trouble really starts. For this reason Illustration 3-18 would be a better interpretation because the children will be blowing over the whole note on into the next measure. After the repeat, being sure the whole note is held four full beats will partially assure good tone and intonation up to the very end.

VARIOUS WAYS OF PLAYING LESSON MATERIALS

One of the biggest problems of class instruction is that of not being able to hear individual students. This factor can be offset by several games that can be played during the progress of the lesson.

The method of setting up the class so the teacher can freely walk between each of the rows and each seat in each row allows the teacher to circulate freely among the class members and stand beside various children and observe what they are doing.

Listening to one child play while the rest of the class sits idle is not only wasting the time of the others in the class but if done too often can cause discipline problems. Individual performances should be made of educational value to the others in the class by either using the class as adjudicators or as a demonstration for the others to emulate.

The teacher can call upon individuals to play from time to time to hear the results of their practice and still not force idleness on the rest of the children by having them act as adjudicators. An adjudication sheet will often make for a more positive approach. A vocal criticism given by the children to fellow classmates wastes time and can be very vicious—children can be very unkind to each other. If the class is given adjudication sheets, they will tend to be more attentative during the performances of their classmates and will not be likely to day-dream.

VARIOUS "GAMES"

Assign each member of the class a number. Divide the exercise being played into various segments and number the segments. Start the child who has been designated as number one. At the point in the music that has been designated as segment number two, the child designated as number two, plays. The children should be instructed that there is to be no break in the flow of the melody. Each child becomes a piece in a puzzle that should fit together perfectly—like one person playing.

Added to this the teacher could have one child play all the way through to keep the tempo going. The teacher could be the unifying factor. This is especially good if the teacher plays an instrument different than that of the class.

This method could be used but have the children in the class choose up teams and pit one team against the other. This is especially of value during the first few attempts at this sort of thing. It is difficult to get through this at the first few attempts. The winner will be merely the team that gets all the way through without a break in the rhythmic flow.

This can be done if there are as few as four in a class. In this case the team may merely alternate every two measures. An eight measure piece that is repeated makes for quite a challenge especially if there is a first and second ending.

When dividing the line into phrases for this type of musical game do not always start the segment at the bar line. If the phrase begins with an anacrusis, so too the child should begin with that note. Usually a fourth beat in a 4/4 exercise or after a long note would make for an anacrusis.

Another method that can be used is again by assigning each child a number. This time however, start the entire class going. In the course of the exercise call out a number. The person whose number is called out continues playing while the rest of the class drops out. This person is then allowed to finish the exercise but all must play the last note together. Having all play the last note together makes them follow along with the person playing.

This can be varied if the exercise is long enough by having all the class come in again when the teacher says "all." Again, a number can be called out. Again the class drops out except for the one whose number is called. If a page of exercises is all in the same meter the class could be challenged into playing the entire page, even with differing key signatures.

This idea can be turned around by starting out with one child and as numbers are called out others are added to the performing group.

The teacher can also use: "one in"—"four in"—"one out"—"two in"—"three in"—"four out," etc. This will surely keep everyone on their toes.

The class can be divided into several groups, each group performing a different task. By using this method each person can have his own responsibility even if there are as many as ten in the class.

1. one group or person plays the exercise as written
2.   ″   ″   ″   ″   plays only the rhythm on one tone
3.   ″   ″   ″   ″   claps the basic beat
4.   ″   ″   ″   ″   claps the rhythm
5.   ″   ″   ″   ″   claps in eighth notes
6.   ″   ″   ″   ″   counts the basic beat
7.   ″   ″   ″   ″   counts the rhythm
8.   ″   ″   ″   ″   counts eighth notes
9.   ″   ″   ″   ″   spells the letter names
10.   ″   ″   ″   ″   sings the syllables

For number two above, the teacher could write a *V* or *I* under various measures and let the child "ad lib" on a dominant or tonic chord. This takes a little extra teaching but with an advanced class it may be possible and prove very interesting to all.

The following is a little more elaborate idea:

1. A student plays the first phrase (or first few measures)
2. If he plays the phrase correctly the class immediately repeats it.
3. A second student then plays the next phrase, etc.
4. If the first student plays the phrase incorrectly, the class does not repeat it. The second student plays that first phrase again by himself.
5. If this second student plays it correctly the class repeats it in unison.
6. If three students in succession play the phrase incorrectly the class plays it in unison three or four times very, very slowly until the error is corrected.
7. The next student then proceeds to the next phrase and the routine begins again.

DRILLING EXERCISES

In the foregoing paragraph the statement was made "play it in unison three or four times very, very slowly until the error is corrected." This statement should be clarified a little. Repetition is one of the best methods for learning anything to be sure, but there is a limit within which pure repetition is of no value. A general rule might be that repetition for repetition's sake is only of value within very small limits. Quoting from an earlier statement in the chapter, "practice makes permanent" applies here. After two or three, or perhaps four repetitions, if the problem is not cleared up, other steps must be taken. Further repetition will be of no value. In reality it will be harmful.

The word "practice" should be used sparingly especially in the very early learning careers of the students. This word should be reserved for that process of dissecting items of an exercise to be worked out. The mere playing through of an exercise is not really "practicing" in the true sense of the word. In most method books it is not really necessary to practice because the lessons are so set up as to systematically teach the various technics necessary for each succeeding lesson. However, any error that is made consistently by the class or a few members of the class should be subject of more careful scrutinization. This scrutinization should center on the exact cause of a problem.

In the exercise shown in Illustration 3-7 there occurs in the second measure from the end what would be a problem for a young clarinetist. The movement from second space *A* to first line *E* is a real problem. No amount of repetition is going to improve this spot efficiently.

The process by which this area can be "practiced" is as follows: *First,* the problem involved should be isolated. The problem being the movement from *A* to *E*. Next the problem should be simplified if at all possible. This is done by abstracting it from the book. The teacher can merely write the letters *A* and *E* on the chalk board. *Second,* the finger motion should be exactly described. The children should be asked to determine exactly what motions and what fingers are involved. They should come up with—the first finger is on the *A* key, resting on its side. It has to roll off the *A* key down onto the *E* tone hole at the same time the thumb touches the *F* tone hole.

Several other steps can be taken before even attempting this movement. First, actual playing could take place by moving first from *A* to *G* concentrating on the roll of the first finger off the *A* key. Next, move from *A* to *F*-sharp. This gives the complete movement of that first finger. These movements should be done in rhythm. Begin with a half note, half rest, half note, half rest, remembering to move the finger quickly to the next position as soon as the half note has concluded.

The next step in playing would be to leave out the half rest —all this without the score.

Another step would be to move back to the half note-half rest but move from the *A* to the *E*. After several repetitions of this, if the finger motion is not coming along as should be expected, one may have to back up and start the process with whole notes and whole rests.

After the *A* to *E* half notes are successful, write a *B*-flat on the board in front of the *A*. Now start with *B*-flat and proceed by half notes, half rests to *A* and to *E*. Though this may not seem absolutely necessary it is, if one is to firmly implant the finger motions into the child's technic. Next, erase the *B*-flat and place an *F* after the *E*. Now play the *A* to *E* to *F* with half notes and half rests. This being completed, again add the *B*-flat.

If one has time and desires to more firmly plant this in the child's technic it is advantageous to reduce the half notes, to quarter notes, quarter rests then substract the quarter rests. This four note figure can also be played forward and backward, i.e., *B*-flat to *A* to *E* to *F* to *E* to *A* to *B*-flat and return. It is just as valuable to practice *A* to *E* as it is to move from *E* to *A*.

SOLO PLAYING

Solo playing should be a part of the regular lesson as soon as the class's playing proficiency is such to correctly perform the tunes that are in some of the beginning solo books. There are several books on the market that can be used after but a few weeks of lessons. The use of solos is one way of challenging those students who are being held back by the class work. Periodically a class will be devoted to each class member performing his solo, with piano accompaniment before the class. Perhaps the piano teacher may even be persuaded to supply an accompanist from her students for just such occasions. If there is an auditorium available by all means make use of it. The children in the class, even if there are only four or five would sit in the audience while their classmate plays from the center of the stage.

This solo playing also makes available at any moment a group of students ready to play for P.T.A., school assemblies, service clubs, etc. It is not always necessary to have the most advanced players perform for groups like this. Those doing well after but a few months of lessons are an excellent advertisement of the program and shows how effective the program is even on the lowest level.

4

Creating Lasting Musicianship Through Technic Classes

This is the portion of the program where the groundwork of future musicianship is laid. The concept of this class is for the dissemination of knowledge that too often is brushed over lightly or neglected entirely in the rush to play tunes. It allows for additional teacher contact time and yet is not just another lesson. Some playing may be done however. It also conserves teacher time because several classes can be met at one time.

Similar instruments may be met together, depending upon the number of classes of each kind of instrument. If there are four classes of cornets with six in each class, all four classes will meet in one technic class. If there are two classes of cornets, two of trombones and one of French horns, these can be combined. The tubas and euphoniums can all be met together. If it is a small school all the brasses and all the woodwinds could be combined into two technic classes. Percussionists could be combined with the brass if absolutely nothing else is possible. It would be better, however, no matter how few percussionists there are, to meet them separately. With percussionists, one lesson could be devoted to work on the practice pad and the technic class devoted to the other percussion instruments concentrating at the outset on the keyboard percussion.

Things that should be taught the beginning instrumentalists, along with fingering their instruments and playing the notes, include care of the instrument and putting it together properly (of particular importance to clarinetists). Such items as terminology need considerable discussion if the children are to really understand all that surrounds the notes.

During the thirty minute lesson there is little time available to discuss the various methods of practicing. The classes should be thoroughly drilled in hand position and versed in the correct method of articulation and breathing. The well informed student should have a knowledge of the workings of his particular instrument. He should know what makes his instrument sound, why the lips must buzz or why sometimes the reed squeaks. There is of course the matter of intonation and phrasing, among others.

We have designated this section of the band program as the "technic class." Actually the "lesson" is really the "technic class" for this is where the children apply the technics they learn. This "technic class" is really the lesson—the time when they learn the things that must be applied to their instruments. This terminology is used in this way because most people, particularly administrators, understand the term "lesson" as the time when the children play their instruments so we shall retain this terminology herein.

For purposes of the discussion herein, some of the information will only cover that portion typical of a clarinet technic class. This therefore is meant only as a guide in establishing those things that are of importance to the beginning band program in general. Also, the discussions herein are not organized in an order that might be most beneficial in every circumstance. Depending upon the method book being used, it may be deemed advisable to take up one or the other of the subjects in a different order. After the selection of a method book for a particular class, the teacher should be able to assemble the various discussions in some kind of logical order and add others that may be in keeping with the progress or the discussion indicated by the method book itself.

The concept of this class is to take some of the weight of information off the class lesson time. It is therefore advantageous for the teacher to take some of the information in the "Outline for Teaching Clarinet to Beginners" (Chapter 2) and move it over into the technic class. Some of the topics to be taken up in the technic class would include: class procedure, basic parts of the clarinet, the reed, mouthpiece, things to remember, troubles in blowing, assembling and disassembling the instrument.

CARE OF INSTRUMENTS

One of the first groups of discussions to be taken up by the teacher in the technic class would be the care of the instruments, including proper methods of handling and cleaning.

The following is a list of items that can be dictated to the children for recording in their notebooks, or given out in mimeographed form and discussed.

1. Always handle the instrument as though it were made out of glass.
2. Give it the care and respect due a treasured possession.
3. Use it only as a musical instrument—never for any other purpose. (see "A Dozen Don'ts!"—Chapter 2)
4. Always keep the instrument in its case when not in use.
5. When in its case, keep it in such a place that it will not get knocked around, shoved, kicked or otherwise battered.
6. If the instrument is momentarily not being played, hold unto it with at least one hand. If it must be laid down, put the case on a flat surface, preferably a table, and lay the instrument in the case.
7. Never lay it on a chair, the floor, a table or music stand.
8. Never stand it on its bell unless it is to be held onto by one hand.
9. Keep the inside and outside of the instrument clean.
10. Eating immediately before playing will tend to allow particles of food to become lodged inside the instrument.

11. Chewing gum while playing or immediately before allows sugar to accumulate on the inside of the instrument.
12. If the keys are wiped off regularly they will keep their shine.
13. Keep the inside of the case clean and free of lint.
14. Always carry the case by its handles. Be sure the handles are secure however.
15. Do not swing the case around or toss it to and fro.
16. Only carry those things in the case for which space is provided.
17. Do not force the lid shut on the case that is crammed with music and other things.
18. Never leave the instrument in a car or trunk in the summer time as the temperature can rise to as much as 170 or 180 degrees.
19. This instrument is your personal responsibility. Only you should handle it. Keep it out of the hands and particularly mouths of other persons who might unwittingly use it improperly and cause damage to be done to it.
20. If problems should arise, seek assistance only from a professional repair man or the instrumental teacher. Relatives and friends are asked not to give assistance as it might only tend to do more harm than that which has already occured.

CARE OF PARTICULAR INSTRUMENTS

After the dissemination of the above information, the technic class should go thoroughly into the cleaning and care of particular instruments. The brass must be taught to clean the insides of their instruments periodically. Mouthpieces too must be cleaned regularly. The following is a list of particulars that should be taught to a typical clarinet technic class. Similar information referring to different instruments should be given out to the other technic classes.

1. Protect the instrument from excessive dryness as it can cause cracking. Hot, dry rooms in winter should be avoid-

ed. Do not leave the instrument near a radiator or hot air register. When wood instruments become very dry, retaining rings may come loose. These rings are put on instruments to keep the thin-walled tenon receivers from cracking when the instrument is assembled. They should be put on and tightened by a repair man immediately.

2. The clarinet must also be protected from excessive moisture. This too can lead to cracking. This may be prevented by swabbing out the instrument after each playing.
   a. The swab should be pulled slowly through the instrument from the bottom up.
   b. Before swabbing, remove the mouthpiece, turn the instrument upside down and slide the weighted end of the swab down the inside of the bore. Do not drop the weighted end down as it may dent the register vent that protrudes into the bore.
   c. Pull the swab through the instrument at least two times.
   d. After disassembling the instrument and placing the pieces in the case, wipe any moisture that may have accumulated out of the tenon receivers.

3. Clean the open tone holes with a solution of castile soap and warm water. This should be done at least twice a year or whenever the holes become corroded.
   a. Saturate a doubled-up pipe cleaner or Q-tip with the soap and water solution and rub the inside of the tone hole. Do not allow water to run down the instrument.
   b. Wipe the tone hole with clean, cold water.
   c. Then wipe the tone hole dry with another doubled-up pipe cleaner or Q-tip.

4. Great care must be taken not to mar the facing of the mouthpiece. It must be kept free of scratches on the inside and chips around the edges. For this reason, always put the cap on the mouthpiece whenever it is not being played. Because the surfaces are so very important to the entire clarinet's responsiveness, the swab must not be pulled through the mouthpiece. It should only be dried out by running a clean handkerchief through it periodically—not after every playing. As it is not made of wood but rod rubber in most cases, drying it out after each playing is not absolutely neces-

sary. However, it should be cleaned thoroughly at least once a week. Do it just before the day of your lesson.

   a. To clean the mouthpiece, simply run lukewarm water through it and then dry it out with a clean handkerchief.

5. Never try to shine the keys with silver polish. This usually results in getting polish on the pads which will cause them not to seat properly. The polish may also get between the posts and rods causing them to work sluggishly. A silver polishing cloth may be used for the keys, provided lint is not allowed to collect on the springs, pads and moving joints.

6. Twice a year the instrument should be cleaned as follows (or more often if necessary):

   a. Clean all dust from under the keys with a pipe cleaner

   b. Wipe out the tone holes with a damp pipe cleaner.

   c. Clean corks and tenon receivers as follows:

      (1) Place some vaseline on a cloth and rub the corks clean

      (2) With the same cloth wipe out the tenon receivers— get way down into the corners. (Use a toothpick ever so gently if necessary.)

      (3) Now wipe with a dry cloth

      (4) Replace with fresh cork grease

   d. With a clothes brush, clean all dirt and lint out of the interior of the case.

HAND POSITION

Hand position is another of those seemingly minor points that can be overlooked, except for a brief reference in the rush to get the class to play tunes. Some concentrated instruction in this area can act as preventive medicine, waylaying future problems. This is just as true in the case of the brass as it is of the woodwinds. As far as the percussionists are concerned, the major portion of the first lessons must be spent on this subject alone. Many a sloppy cornet player can trace his troubles to habits built up over a period of years by allowing the fingers to lay well over the valves or lifted high above the valve buttons.

As with the other discussions herein, the following is an outline of work on hand position and its related details for a typical clarinet technic class.

Left Hand

1. The left thumb is placed on the thumb ring overlapping it so as to be in close contact with the register key. The angle of the thumb is about 30 degrees below horizontal in relation to the body of the clarinet.
   a. The thumb should not shift its position to open the register key.
   b. Be sure the thumb does not fall parallel to the clarinetist's body.
2. The first finger is curved slightly at each joint, and points downward slightly.
   a. The first joint must be close to the *A* key.
   b. The second joint must be close to the *A*-flat key.
3. The second finger assumes a similar angle on the *D* ring as that of the first finger.
4. The third finger reaches downward to the *C* tone hole. It will approach this tone at a slight angle as did the first and second finger.
5. The fourth or little finger is practically straight as it contacts the *E-B* key.

Left Arm

The left arm should be held slightly away from the side of the body with the inside elbow joint approximately three inches from the body.

Practice Without the Clarinet

1. Hold the arm out horizontally with the palm facing down-

ward, the elbow three inches from the side; fingers relaxed and slightly curved; wrist straight.

    a. Observe the natural line at the wrist joint

        (1) It is almost on a level with the forearm rising only slightly to the knuckles

2. Turn the palm inward
3. Swing the hand and lower arm inward from the elbow joint

    a. Observe the natural shape of the hands and fingers as they approach the position for clarinet fingering

Right Hand (for Beginning Tones)

1. The first finger is placed under the thumb rest
2. The thumb is placed on top of the thumb rest

Right hand—to be given when the note *B* (two spaces below the staff) is introduced or for silent practice purposes.

1. The right thumb supports the weight of the instrument. The thumb rest lies on the side of the thumb in line with the base of the thumb nail.

    a. Be sure the thumb rest is not placed too far to the right, resting in the crotch of the thumb and first finger.

2. The first finger is curved slightly at each joint, and points slightly downward to the B-flat tone hole.

    a. If the hand is held without a bend in the wrist, the fingers do not and should not touch the side trill keys. If the fingers do touch the side trill keys, the wrist should be lowered.

        (1) This is especially a problem for a very young child with a small hand.

3. The second and third fingers assume a similar position as the first finger on their respective tone holes.

The natural pads of the fingers, not the finger tips are used to close the holes and operate the keys.

Silent Practice

This should be done by a silent placing of the left thumb

across the thumb hole and the fingers in an orderly T-1-2-3-4-5-plan.

1. First, this should be done by the children resting the bell on their knee and watching the fingers.
2. Then do it with the eyes closed
    a. The correct position is important and the holes should be covered naturally and with as relaxed a feeling as possible.
3. The students should be instructed to finger as follows:
    "Thumb—1—Thumb"
    "Thumb—1—2—1—Thumb"
    "Thumb—1—2—3—2—1—Thumb"
    Do this first one at a time then in rhythmic sequence.

It is a good practice to keep the right hand little finger in close proximity if not actually touching the *F/C* key and the left hand little finger on the *E/B* key. This prevents the curling of the little fingers under the hand, into the palm, putting a strain on the third fingers and developing a bad habit.

REEDS

All too often a child will go to a music store, purchase one or two reeds and attempt to play on them. Most times the reeds will be too hard for the beginner, even though the store clerk took them out of a box marked "medium" or "medium soft." Any clarinetist will testify to the fact that an entire box of reeds marked "medium" could conceivably have but two reeds out of the twenty-four that would match up to the player's idea of what a "medium" strength reed should be. Other reeds in the box can range from very, very soft to very, very hard.

A beginning clarinet player has enough trouble without adding this to his list of obstacles—reeds that don't work properly for him. A word should be said in defense of the reed manufacturers however. There is really no way to test the strength of a reed except by playing it on the instrument it is to be used upon. Many factors are involved in the strength of a reed when blown upon. Such things as the instrument itself, the mouthpiece, its facing and demensions, even the individual's embouchure can make one reed that feels medium to one player seem medium hard or even hard to another.

Thus it is best for the teacher to secure, test and distribute the first two or three reeds that will be used by the beginning clarinetists. Though it is time consuming, it is the only way one can be even partially sure the proper strength reed is being used. This is only partial certainty for the children's individual embouchures will vary as will the cane itself as it is used.

At the earliest convenient time the clarinet technic class should spend time discussing the selection and adjustment of reeds.

SELECTION OF THE REED

Hold the reed up to the light.

1. The light should pass thru the tip of the reed exposing an inverted "V" with a rounded point somewhat like a "U".
2. The sides of the reed should show light approximately the same distance down the reed.
3. Make certain that the reed does not show light the same distance down the middle of the reed as this indicates that the heart of the reed has been cut away.
4. The left side of the reed may be slightly heavier than the right side.
5. Good reeds will have noticeable grain lines. These lines should be distributed evenly in the reed and should run to the tip of the reed.

Adjusting reeds—use a small pocket knife or fine sandpaper.

1. If the reed is too hard, it is too thick in the section between the tip and stock on the sides.
2. Scrape on the side starting about 3/4 of an inch back from the tip and toward the center of that tip.
   a. Do not scrape the center—only the sides.

    b. The right side should be scraped first as this is the side
that should be a little lighter than the left.

    c. Test by blowing after each scraping.

    d. Take only a very little off at a time.

The teacher should not only give this foregoing information
to the children but should take a reed that is hard and work on
it so they will get an idea of what should be done. He could
also distribute some hard reeds to the class and work them down
to the proper strength together.

As far as a soft reed is concerned this is easily remedied by
using a good reed cutter and having one available for the students to use whenever necessary.

The explanation about scraping the reed is only brief to be
sure but should suffice at this early stage. At some later date the
teacher should go further into the problem and make use of a
publication like *The Art of Adjusting Reeds* by Daniel Bonade,
published by G. Leblanc Corporation of Kenosha, Wisconsin.

POSTURE

Assuming a good posture when playing an instrument may
well be more important mentally than physically. Traditionally
we say that if one does not sit up straight one cannot take in a
full breath and the diaphragm or throat may become restricted
and prevent the even, smooth flow of air necessary for good tone
production. Whereas this may be true it is doubtful if this has
too great an effect on the actual playing of an instrument. It
will be found that if one has a player who slouches and plays
flat, his pitch (in nine out of ten cases) will immediately come
up if he is made to sit up straight.

Psychologically a great many things happen and are directly
related to posture. Rarely does one see a forceful, confident individual walking around with his head down and shoulders
slumped forward. How many politicians running for office
slouch over the lecturn when speaking? They usually seem to

be striving to stand as tall as possible giving those watching and listening a feeling of his own self confidence. Note also a great batter on a baseball team. If he walks up to the plate and takes a slouchy stance one can see he is not going to put the ball over the fence. The greats take a firm-footed stance and look the pitcher straight in the eye. He usually walks up to the plate swinging not just one club but two or three. He does not stroll up dragging his bat behind him in the dirt.

Observe the stance of a great trumpet player. That instrument comes up to his mouth and stands out straight and bold. The child who allows his instrument to almost rest on his chest is admitting defeat. He cannot even hold it out to the world and say: "See, I am master of this tubing." Rather he is saying in essence: "I am not so sure of myself and would rather not play out—maybe if it bounces off the floor it will be better."

Many a clinician has taken an average player out of a band and improved his tone immediately. More often than not it is done simply by getting him to blow into the instrument. Not just with a thin, incipient, apologetic amount of air but strong, vibrant, confident volumes. Notice, if you ever have the opportunity to witness such a metamorphosis that all the time the clinician is forcing up the bell of the instrument by lifting the bell gently with his own hand.

Saxophonists may be the band's worst examples of posture. They take the instrument out of the case, put it together and then adjust their head, neck, arms, and upper torso to fit the instrument. Students must be taught that the saxophone does not go together straight. The mouthpiece, neck pipe and neck strap must be adjusted to fit the player's body—not the other way around. In the case of all saxophones, both the mouthpiece and neck pipe *must* be turned slightly toward the left. The mouthpiece and neck pipe are *not* to be placed in a straight line with the body of the instrument.

Trombonists and flutists too have their instrument enslavement positions. The trombonist admits to the trombone that it is too much for him. He does it by holding it in such a way that the slide almost hits the floor when he reaches for the seventh position. The flutist gives in to the flute even before he has learned all the notes. There is a need for a slight bending of the head to the right but it should be only slight. Allowing the young flutist to rest his arm on the back of the chair to hold it up is saying: "You are too much for me. I have to use the chair as a crutch."

Most chairs are not really made for humans to sit on. Most children in the lower grades, when coming to the band room for their lessons, have to sit on chairs that are usually occupied by the older band members. These "upstarts" on the road to the band cannot even touch the floor if they sit all the way back on the chair. Instead of letting their feet dangle, they must be taught to sit forward and plant their feet solidly on the floor.

Rather than simply telling the child to sit up, some rules should be laid down as just how to do this. The following may help get them off to a good start:

1. Sit so that both feet can rest squarely on the floor.
   a. It will be found that the most comfortable position is one whereby the feet are placed about six or eight inches apart with the right slightly ahead of the left.
2. Sit as far back on the chair as is possible (remembering the feet must touch the floor) .
   a. A short person will not be able to touch the back of the chair.
   b. Only if the person is large enough will his back touch the back of the chair.
3. Sit in such a way that the back bone is arched inward slightly and the shoulders are held high and back.
   a. Do not allow the backbone to sag outward so there is a bending forward of the upper torso.
   b. Pretend there is a rope coming out of the top of the head and is connected to a pully directly above. Sit up as though someone were pulling upon that rope. This should push the shoulders back and pull the stomach in.
4. Being as the instrument is an integral part of the posture each section of the band should be given definite instructions as to the position at which the instrument is to be held.

It is of great importance that the concept of assuming a good posture be started from the beginning for "as a twig is bent so grows the tree."

BREATHING

There are almost as many ways of teaching breathing as there are teachers. Here are a few ways that this item may be taught to instrumentalists. Several ideas are given herein, not to show the divergence of opinion but to encourage teachers that if "at first you don't succeed" you are running about average. A teacher should have several ideas at hand so if one does not work another might.

There does seem to be two divergent views of attack in this matter. Some attack it from the diaphragm support angle. This involves an understanding of the diaphragm and its function. Others approach it from the tone angle. This last group contends that if the tone is good then diaphragmatic action must be correct. Both camps however, agree if the tone is not good some care must be taken to teach the proper methods of breathing and blowing.

Barry M. Shank writes:[1] The exhaling process is the most important breathing facet in playing, since it is blowing which produces the sound. . . . Disregard the mental concept of the diaphragm or lower areas of breathing. Think of blowing directly thru the horn. Projection! A good singer does not imagine 'pushing' with his diaphragm or, as he sings, tightening his abdominal muscles. What does he do? A trained singer takes advantage of his frontal resonating chambers in order to produce a big, resonant, articulate sound. (Wind) players are no different. They also must make use of the facial bone structure. This is the mental concept that should be taught young . . . players. Thus, no discussion of diaphragm expansion really is necessary. If you blow properly out front, the breath ap-

---

[1]The following material, through page 109, is from Barry M. Shank, "Short Cut to Correct Breathing." *The Instrumentalist*, XVIII, 3 (October, 1963), 30.

paratus works automatically! A major effort should be concentrated on blowing the air from the mouth thru the horn.
Have the feeling of blowing your nose. Feel the pressure of
the air against the front of the face. . . ."

Three steps are utilized in developing (this idea):

Step 1. Start "frontal projection" by developing a vocal "m"
sound or hum that vibrates the entire nasal bone
structure of the face. (Of course, it is possible to hum
without good frontal projection, but this will require careful instruction.)

Step 2. Using a well-developed frontal hum, open the lips
into a pucker whistle position and begin to whistle.
This sounds rather complex, but what results here is
the coordination of a good frontal projection with the
release of air. You are gradually moving towards playing the instrument.

Step 3. This step, a "buzz card" technic, adds a vibrating medium to the air stream. Any small card will suffice.
While doing the hum and whistle, place the end of
the card against the open lips, making the card vibrate sympathetically with the sounds. The more
center of sound there is to the buzz on the card, the
greater the degree of frontal projection.

Many teachers suggest that students be taught breathing exercises. Here are two such ideas:

In *The Art of Saxophone Playing*, Larry Teal suggests this
exercise in proper breathing:

1. Walk slowly, keeping the body loose.
2. Stand erect, but comfortably. Shoulders and arms should be
relaxed. Swing the arms while walking.
3. Take in a full breath quickly, on one step.
4. Hold this breath for two steps.
5. Exhale through the mouth slowly for eight to ten steps.
6. Take two more steps before the next inhalation.

You will notice that, in the above exercise, the inhalation is
fast and the remainder of the cycle is much slower.[2]

---

[2]Larry Teal, *The Art of Saxophone Playing.* copyright © 1963 by Summy-
Birchard Co., Evanston, Illinois. All rights reserved. Used by permission.

The next series of exercises are suggested by Frederick Wilkins:[3]

These are helpful for the development of breath control and should be practiced daily with regularity. Increase gradually from ten to twenty times a day, or more. If fatigued, do not exceed six times without a rest period.

EXERCISE A

1. Place palm of hand upon the abdomen just below the ribs.
2. Take a breath slowly, feeling the diaphragm move outward against the hand.
3. Still inhaling slowly, expand the chest upward and outward until a comfortable supply of air has been taken.
4. Hold the breath for several seconds.
5. Exhale slowly, but do not permit the ribs to contract until almost all the air has been expelled.
6. The diaphragm does not retract until the end of the exhalation.

In performing this exercise, always remember that the breath must flow out evenly. If the result is jerky and wavering, inhale a smaller quantity of air and the control of it will be easier. The beginner can hear the out-flow of air if he will use the sibilant "S" when exhaling. It is advisable for him to do this in all the exercises so that he can tell if the breath is flowing smoothly and steadily. As he gains control of the breath, he should increase the inhalation.

EXERCISE B

1. Inhale, following the first 3 steps as explained in Exercise A.
2. Exhale slowly, interrupting the steady flow of air by frequent pauses.

The purpose of these pauses is to strengthen the muscles used in controlling the air column.

EXERCISE C

1. Inhale slowly.

---

[3]Frederick Wilkins, "The Mechanics of Breathing". *The Conn Chord*, VI, 3, (May, 1963), 12.

2. Hold breath for several counts when capacity is reached.
3. Exhale quickly.

EXERCISE D

1. Inhale quickly.
2. When the lung capacity is reached, hold the breath again.
3. Exhale slowly and steadily.

PRACTICE

Most teachers are concerned with the amount and frequency with which children practice. The method by which the students practice should also be considered. Just as the lesson is for teaching the children how to blow, finger and read notes, the technic class can be used for teaching the children how to practice.

The first consideration, however, would be merely to get the children to practice every day. One of the greatest aids to assure this is through the use of practice cards. Many of the instrument manufacturers have printed cards which can be secured free or at a very minimal cost. These records give a clear view of the child's work in this area. They are an effective means of goading indifferent students into becoming practice-conscious. Since the parents must initial most forms the week's work provides for some communication between the parent and child.

Illustrations 4-1 and 4-2 are simple sheets that could be run off on a mimeograph machine. Illustration 4-1 is a monthly report, set up like a monthly calendar. The children would enter the dates in the corner of one box and their practice time. Illustration 4-2 would be passed out weekly and slipped into the lesson book like a book mark. The children could also be instructed to purchase from the book store or office supply a pocket sized date book and merely enter the practice time in the spaces normally used for entering appointments.

Illustrations 4-3 and 4-4 are some of the many types of published materials that appear in booklet form. These practice records also provide the teacher with space for recording the materials for the lesson. These, it is true are designed for use in private lessons but could be utilized with classes as well. With class lessons the children would be expected to enter for themselves the lesson assignments.

ILLUSTRATION 4-1

Student's Name						
Sun.	Mon.	Tues.	Wed.	Thurs.	Fri.	Sat.

ILLUSTRATION 4-2

Student's Name						
Sun.	Mon.	Tues.	Wed.	Thurs.	Fri.	Sat.

Parent Signature _____

Illustration 4-3[4] is one that has a staff for special work or scales that may be assigned.

Illustration 4-4[5] has the practice record and lesson assignment on one page and across from it six staves for recording whatever information the teacher may desire.

ILLUSTRATION 4-3

PERIOD: FROM_____ TO_____

LESSON ASSIGNMENT:

PRACTICE RECORD	
M	
T	
W	
T	
F	
S	
TOTAL	

---

[4]*Wright-Way Practice Record.* Witchita, Kansas: Milo Wright, 28 pp.
[5]Elizabeth Brient Smith, *The Little Music Book* (San Antonio, Texas: Southern Music Co., 1956), 45 pp.

ILLUSTRATION 4-4

	Grades + or –	
Date		Lesson No.

New Piece	Technic
Scale	
Cadence	
	Special Study
Other Pieces	
Scales	
Cadences	Keyboard Harmony
	Theory Drills
	Sight Reading

PRACTISE			PRACTISE		
Monday	Tuesday	Wednesday	Thursday	Friday	Saturday
Repertoire			Bulletin Board		
		Lesson Grade			

LENGTH OF PRACTICE PERIOD

The length of time a student practices varies with the degree of advancement. Directives with regards to the length of time they should spend practicing should be given to the children and their parents so that no misunderstandings will arise. At the very beginning the children should be encouraged to practice 30 minutes but perhaps in three separate sessions of 10 minutes each. By the time the children reach sixth grade a thirty to forty-five minute practice period should be expected.

HOW TO PRACTICE

1. Select a time of day that will be as free as possible from interruptions and try to use that time every day.
2. Choose a place where there will be freedom from distractions.
3. Have the lesson objectives in mind. Decide upon some things that should be accomplished. (It is not necessary to play every measure and every note of the lesson at each practice session.)
4. Be self critical. Criticisms must be in objective terms, however.
5. Isolate troublesome passages and work on them.
   a. Reduce the speed, keeping all elements under complete control until the desired standard of excellence is achieved then increase the speed to that which is necessary for proper performance. This may take weeks.
   b. The secret to correct playing may be summed up in one simple four-lettered word—SLOW, not quite slow, not very slow, but very, very, very slow!
6. Repetition is one of the means to correct progress but only

if the repetition itself is correct. Learn it first slowly, then
secure that technic by correct repetition.

7. Do not just play—practice.

REMEMBER: Practice makes perfect only when the practice
is perfect!

The following is a dialogue by Marjorie Bram that one can
use to introduce the children to an approach to proper ideas of
practicing:

"I'm you, I'm home, and I'm holding my instrument like
this," you announce, making a gigantic and successful attempt
to look grotesque. "What am I doing wrong? Fix me." The class
will be only too glad to, giggling in the process but getting the
message loud and clear. Immediate result: sharper perception,
stimulated consciousness, and cultivation of objectivity.

"I'm you, I'm home, and I play a note that comes out like
this." You demonstrate, sounding like Donald Duck. "Why?"
you ask the students, and you follow all supposedly correct suggestions, valid or not, until you can ask for the last time, "Is
that a good sound now?" and get a gleeful and unanimous
"Yes!" Another—"Why (is it good now) ?" clinches it. Result:
awareness of good tone quality, and ways of attaining it.

"How does this sound to you?" You've pointed out the passage in the method book which you're going to play, and now
you make a deliberate mistake or two, perhaps throwing in a
bad sound or a posture flaw for good measure. Let them evaluate. ("Evaluate" is a less negative, less frightening word than
"criticize.") Cultivate in them the habit of saying first what's
good, and follow with what's not good. Teach with a pleasant
humor and positive thinking. Result: improving is fun, and
standards rise!

In relation to many situations like the three just described,
we should remember that there is no wasted experience. If we
aren't learning what to do, we can, at the same moment, be
learning what not to do. Moments like these are indeed very
well spent.[6]

---

[6]Marjorie Bram, "Do We Teach Them to Practice?" *The Instrumentalist*,
XXII, 3, (October 1967), 30.

A HINT FOR PRACTICING

Leopold Mozart made practicing a game for his young son, Wolfgang. He placed ten peas in young Mozart's pocket and each time a passage was played perfectly, Wolfgang removed a pea and placed it in a second pocket. If a mistake was made however, all the peas were returned to the original pocket and the passage played until it had been played perfectly ten times in a row and the peas were all in the second pocket.

Perhaps for the fifth grader, five pennies could be used rather than ten peas. Ten perfect performances of a single exercise may be a little too much to expect but would make for an interesting challenge.

WHAT MAKES FOR GOOD MUSICIANSHIP?

What does a student look for when practicing? What things must a student do to be able to claim he is playing an exercise correctly? What things must be done to be able to claim he has played an exercise perfectly? A simple answer would be: "Play all those things that are on the score!" But, just what are those things that are on the score that one is supposed to observe?

To play everything that is on the score is easy to say but more direct explanation should be included if the children are to be expected to understand exactly what is to be done.

The *Watkins-Farnum Performance Scale* is a set of fourteen rather short (some only sixteen measures in length) musical examples. These musical examples range from the very simple containing only half and whole notes to the very, very difficult with tempos up to $\bullet\!\!\text{.} = 132$ and $\bullet\!\!\text{.} = 60$, containing a profusion of dynamics, slurs, ties, wide range and tempo changes.

These are designed for testing instrumentalists' playing ability from six months of lessons up to six years. The preliminary text includes a description of what constitutes errors in playing for purposes of grading the performance of these exercises. This list of errors make an excellent group of topics for discussion and demonstration during the technic class.

Dr. John G. Watkins and Dr. Stephen E. Farnum set down the following items that are to be considered as errors on the performance scale:

1. Pitch errors
   a. A tone added or a tone omitted constitutes an error.
   b. A tone played on the wrong pitch is an error.
2. Time errors
   a. Any note not given its correct value
3. Change of time errors
   a. If there is a marked increase or decrease in tempo, all measures played in the incorrect tempo are wrong.
4. Expression errors
   a. Failure to observe any expression marks constitutes an error (these include forte and piano markings, crescendo, decrescendo, accelerando, ritardando, etc.)
5. Slur errors
   a. A slur omitted, a tongued note slurred, a slur carried onto notes which should be tongued, or a broken slur are counted as errors.
6. Rests
   a. Ignoring a rest or failure to give a rest its correct value is an error.
7. Holds and pauses
   a. Holds written thus ⌒ should be treated (properly)

   (Pauses between notes within the measure are to be counted as errors.)
8. Repeats
   a. (Repeat signs must be observed.) [7]

---

[7]Joseph G. Watkins and Stephen E. Farnum, "Types of Errors," *The Watkins-Farnum Performance Scale.* Winona, Minnesota: Hal Leonard Music, Inc., 1954. p 6.

THEORY

The continuation of the knowledge of letter names, rhythmic notation, and terminology can be enlarged by using various types of work books. There are many such work books being published specifically for use with elementary band students. This theory can also be enlarged to cover some discussions of elementary acoustics as well.

SIMPLE ACOUSTICS

A discussion might begin by posing the following questions: What is sound? What makes some sounds higher than others? Can you see sound? What is the difference between a musical tone and noise?

Sound is the sensation of hearing that is picked up by the ear drum and transmitted to the brain. A vibrating medium (like the reed on a clarinet) is transmitted through the air and sets the ear drum vibrating in a similar fashion. The word vibration merely means the rapid wiggling back and forth of an object (the scientific term for this wiggling is oscillation).

One can see sound by observing the lowest string on a string bass when it is plucked or the low strings on a piano when the key is depressed. The effects of vibrations (the source of sound) can also be seen if a small bit of paper is placed on the head of a timpani and the head struck with a mallet. (The small bit of paper will jump all around). A simple device to show what vibrations are can be constructed merely by securing a small wooden box or cardboard box with sturdy sides and stretching a rubber band around it. Plucking the rubber band will set it in a very slow vibration (provided it is a big enough rubber band).

The vibrations of the low string bass strings or the low piano strings or the rubber band are very, very slow indeed. If these strings were tightened, the vibrations would become much faster. As they (or any string) becomes tighter and the speed increases, the eye may no longer be able to see it move. Also, one will notice that the pitch will rise. It should therefore be noted that the slower the speed of vibration the lower the pitch or frequency. As the tension increases, the speed increases and the pitch rises.

Vibrations are spoken of in relation to the number of oscillations per second. Most everyone who plays an instrument for any length of time becomes familiar with the expression: A-440. This means that the note *A* (second space of the treble clef) should emit 440 vibrations per second. If a string or an oboe emits 448 vibrations per second this pitch would be higher than the standardized note *A* and thus said to be "sharp." If all instruments are to play well together, they must sound each note with the same number of vibrations. For this reason the A-440 has been established. Even though the eye cannot see and count these extremely fast vibrations, scientists can count them by electronic means. Scientists have devised a machine to count vibrations—it is called an oscilloscope. This gives a picture of what sound looks like and allows the number of vibrations per second to be counted.

If one were to cut a string bass string in half, and greatly slow down it's speed—like putting it on a slow motion movie camera, it would look like the swinging of a pendulum. A pendulum works and acts just like the vibrations of an instrument. If one were then to attach a pencil to the bottom of the pendulum (or slow motion string bass string) and draw it across a piece of paper, while it was swinging, the mark that would be left would look like that shown in Illustration 4-5.

Illustration 4-5 is the picture of what would be a very simple vibration. This is what sound looks like when it moves through the air—only much more rapidly. However, most musical sounds would not produce such a simple sound wave pattern. A real

ILLUSTRATION 4-5

sound wave pattern is made up of many smaller tones mixed in with the larger one. These smaller tones are called "overtones." The more complicated sound wave then might look like Illustration 4-6.

Even though the pattern is not simple, it nevertheless presents an even pattern that is repeated over and over again. This pattern is said to be that of a musical tone. If the wave pattern that is emitted were to form a really scattered effect (that is, one that does not appear to have any discernible pattern) then it is considered to be noise. A wave pattern for noise might look like Illustration 4-7.

Obviously this is just a cursory glance at the subject, but it could be amplified according to the age and experience of the pupils. As they progress, introduce new materials with the cor-

ILLUSTRATION 4-6

ILLUSTRATION 4-7

rect vocabulary. Making sure the students know the physical properties of their instruments and its many mechanical defects will help them to realize how much is dependent upon their own musical perception to play in tune.

As the squeaks of the reeds, the overblown octaves of the flute, the harmonics of the strings, and the overly tense embouchure of the brasses make their inevitable appearances, the instructor should give a good physical reason why they happen. What is even more important than the reason they occur is *what the student must do to correct his errors.* Remember, this is a strange and unfamiliar piece of equipment to the student. The sooner he understands his instrument so that it becomes second nature to him the better he will play.

AN AID TO INTONATION

One of the quickest purposes for which the acoustical information can be used is in tuning. Assuming there is no electronic equipment (Stroboscope) to show visual correction, demonstrate to the students what causes two tones to sound out of tune, and how this can be corrected.

This can be done by explaining about the special cause of interference causing beats. Beats occur when two wave trains of slightly different frequencies sound at the same time causing a pulsation of tone. In other words, the two wave trains literally bump into each other. This can easily be demonstrated on the chalk board by drawing two parallel wave trains, and showing their possible collision.

Show how instruments can be tuned to each other by various physical adjustments until the wave trains merge in phase. This is an important first step in having students learn to play in tune within the ensemble.[8]

[8]James Riley, "Sound Simplified," *The Instrumentalist,* XII, 9, (May, 1958), p 25.

5

Establishing Trouble-Free Relations with Parents

Parent contact is first made with the sending home of forms for the children to join the pre-band program (if one is offered). It is continued through the reporting of the progress the children made in the pre-band program. Contact is further continued through the change-over period (from the pre-band class to real instruments) and the reporting of results of the aptitude test.

Because of the excitement of playing in a band and the newness of the instruments, the first two weeks of beginning band are not too much of a problem, especially if the band is established on a firm pre-school band program. It will be after about three or four weeks that problems begin to arise. A little moral support for all concerned is sometimes needed. Information like that shown in Illustrations 5-1, 5-2 and 5-3 may be of great help in this situation.

A personal contact with parents may also be possible during this beginning band period. If the school's P.T.A. is having a meeting, the parents of beginning instrumentalists could be notified that the instrumental teacher will be on hand at the conclusion of the meeting to answer any questions that parents might have. The P.T.A. president is usually only too happy to

ILLUSTRATION 5-1

Dear Parent:

Learning to play a band instrument is not easy--but can be enjoyable after a few months of HARD WORK.

Instrumental music teachers have long recognized the value of sympathetic encouragement from the home. As you hear the results of your child's first lessons and ask (under your breath), "Is it supposed to sound like that?", stop and consider the challenges your child has accepted. As he attempts to play he is expected to think of all the following things at once:

1. Associate note names, values, key and fingers with the printed score

2. Breathe and blow in a consciously controlled manner

3. Control the tongue and lips to start and sustain each tone

4. Adhere to the rhythm patterns indicated by the meter signature

5. Place the proper fingers on the proper keys, rings, or valves to produce the pitches called for by the score

If any of these steps are not done correctly, your youngster may very well experience difficulties that will retard his progress and as a result, can easily discourage him.

Since you have consented to your child's playing an instrument, I assume that you believe his playing to have real value as a part of his growing up, and later, as part of his life as an adult. You have seen from the demands listed above there are going to be some rough moments in that you will have to beg or coerce him to practice. The axiom "perseverance pays" certainly applies to the budding instrumentalist. Through psychological, and even physiological persuasion, you have taught him to brush his teeth, comb his hair, drink his milk and wash his face. You did not say to yourself, "If he doesn't want to, I'll be darned if I'll push him." You said, "I do these things because I know that someday he will see the value in them, just as I do now." I sincerely hope you will remember this when the going gets a little tough.

Please feel free to call me at school or at my home if at any time a problem arises. We have a common interest--your youngster.

Sincerely,

Band Director

ILLUSTRATION 5-2

SINCE 1892

PEATE'S MUSIC HOUSE. INC.

VIOLIN MAKERS AND IMPORTERS

FRANKLIN SQ. • UTICA NEW YORK • TELEPHONE RANDOLPH 4-6615

Congratulations to you! Your child is now studying a musical instrument and is embarking on a musical path which will surely enrich his or her life in many ways

We know that beginning students sometimes have difficulty in properly handling their instruments during the first few weeks, and yet it is especially important during this time to have an instrument which is in perfect playing condition. We have, therefore, made arrangements with your music instructor to check your child's instrument and make any necessary adjustments. It may be necessary to bring some instruments into our repair shop overnight for these adjustments. There is no charge for this service for our prime concern is that the musical instrument which your child is now playing be in top playing condition.

It is common, at this stage, for some doubts to creep into the mind of the student as to his musical ability . . . for the first few weeks are indeed difficult. "Wrong notes" are expected at this time and the encouragement and praise of the parents is not only welcome but can be the most important factor in your child's success. The enclosed brochure is for your young musician - it may also help to encourage him.

Please don't hesitate to call us if you have any problems or questions about the program.

Sincerely yours,

PEATE'S MUSIC HOUSE, INC.

Paul D. Williams

ILLUSTRATION 5-3

cooperate with any part of the school program. He might even include information about the possibility of getting a few extra parents out for the meeting. The instrumental teacher of course should not take advantage of the situation. Be sure that the parents meet with the teacher *after* the P.T.A. meeting. And, the instrumental teacher should not time his arrival at school just as the meeting is concluding. It would not hurt if he were in attendance at the entire meeting.

During this time the parents should also be kept informed as to the progress or lack of progress their child is making. Illustrations 5-4, 5-5 and 5-6[1] are examples of reports that can be sent home.

They should also be informed just when the rental program will expire if such should be occurring in the near future. Illustration 5-7 is such a letter designed for this purpose.

TALK TO PARENTS

The talk to parents will consist of discussions about the instruments, whether or not they should purchase one, the quality they should look for, and additional aids that will help their child be successful in his efforts to become a member of the band.

By the time of this meeting the parents will have been informed as to whether their child should continue playing. The parents will need to be reassured that their investment in time and money will not be wasted. This meeting should offer ample opportunity for parents to bring up any questions. Pieces of paper might be passed out as the parents enter the meeting so they can write down any questions they might have. These then should be answered by the instrument teacher or instrument company representative. The person in charge of the meeting could say: "Please write down even the most ridiculous ques-

---

[1]Hal Thorley, "Postcard to Parents." *The Instrumentalist*, XIV, 10, (June, 1960), 4.

ILLUSTRATION 5-4

Dear Parent,

It has been _____ weeks since your child, _____,
began instrumental lessons. Up to this point _____ is:

_____ doing very well, ahead of the class

_____ doing average work, keeping up with the class

_____ falling behind the rest of the class because:

_____ needs more practice at home

_____ needs more encouragement at home

_____ shows no interest

Remarks:

I am sure you are interested in your child's progress and hope
you will feel free to call me if you have any questions regarding the instrumental music program.

                              Sincerely yours,

                              Instrumental Instructor

ILLUSTRATION 5-5

ʄive week report

FOR_____

1	2	3	4	5

Recommended to continue lessons ☐

Not recommended to continue lessons ☐

A = excellent progress
B = progress is very good
C = is making average progress
D = progress not what it should be

X = absent from class at the time the
    report was made out

ILLUSTRATION 5-6

Dear Parent or Guardian:

_____ has not been doing
satisfactory work on his or her instrument.
Please check on the problems indicated below.
With your cooperation the problem may be solved
and improvement in the work will be possible.
Thank you very much.

                            Sincerely yours,

                        _____

1. _____ Instrument is in need of repair.

2. _____ Needs strings, reeds, oil, supplies,
           music, etc.

3. _____ Tardiness to lessons or rehearsals.

4. _____ Absent from lessons.

5. _____ Absent from band rehearsals.

6. _____ Not learning lesson assignments.

7. _____ Has poor attitude in class and is
           uncooperative.

8. _____ Others

ILLUSTRATION 5-7

VIOLIN MAKERS AND IMPORTERS   SINCE 1892

 PEATE'S MUSIC HOUSE, INC.

52 FRANKLIN SQUARE   •   UTICA NEW YORK   •   AREA CODE 315   724-8615

CABLE ADDRESS PEATMUSIC

PAUL D WILLIAMS

This is just a reminder that the trial period for the
your child is now using will expire on   I hope that instrumental music has proven to be a pleasant, helpful and interesting experience for you and your child.

On or before   you may choose to follow any of these alternatives; after consulting with the teacher:

1. Pay the remaining balance of $ thus saving the carrying
   charge of $
2. Pay the additional down payment of $ and ten monthly in-
   stallments thereafter of $ beginning
3. Return the instrument to us in good condition and forfeit the
   $ already paid. $1.00 per day will be charged if instrument is returned after

Our store is located on Franklin Square opposite the Boston Store and
is open from 9:00 to 9:00 on Monday and 9:00 to 5:00 Tuesday through
Saturday.

May we hear from you sometime before the expiration date? We
shall be glad to answer any questions you may have and to help or
assist you in any way we can.

                   Yours sincerely,

                   PEATE'S MUSIC HOUSE, INC.

                   Paul D. Williams

PDW/gm

tions you may think you have. It is only in this way we can really understand and seek the solutions to your problems. Oftentimes, your questions will help others. Certainly they will help us in our efforts to make the band program of greater value to your child."

The program could actually get under way with a statement something like this:

"We have prepared for you several items that should be helpful in securing success for your child in the band program. You already know from hearing your son or daughter practice that it is not going to be easy. We all know too that anything of value in life is only acquired thru hard work. It is hard work that makes life interesting and full—provided there is success that comes out of this hard work. Most of the children in the groups that performed (if a performance is given) already know the feeling that comes from a job well done. I am sure the majority now feel that these past weeks of work have been well worth the effort. Tonight they received, by your applause, a reward that is music to the ears of a musician. A reward that never diminishes. It matters not whether it is received in the elementary school auditorium, the high school auditorium, the civic auditorium, or New York's Carnegie Hall."

PURCHASING INSTRUMENTS

If the school uses a rental-purchase plan, the next discussion may not be of too great an interest or value to the parents because they will no doubt purchase the instrument their child has been using. If a substantial number of children are using school-owned instruments or inferior rented or purchased instruments, the following will then be necessary.

James Robbins has written about the attitude many parents have with regard to purchasing an instrument for their young child.

"ALL THAT GLITTERS IS NOT GOLD" [2]

Dad and Mother went downtown shopping. At the music store they were shown several clarinets. . . . Dad came home in a purple mood. "Over $200.00 for that little stick of black wood; it's a crime!" Mother, who wanted a deep freeze that cost $300.00, also expressed unhappiness. Johnny was told that music was out; his parents would take him to the circus next summer, but it cost too much to buy a clarinet.

Johnny put up quite a fuss and, at length, Dad promised to look further for an instrument. In reading the newspaper that evening, he happened to see the advertisement of a pawn shop. Music instruments were mentioned. The next day he visited the shop and found a genuine Albert system clarinet for only $50.00. The merchant assured him that this was the very best kind of clarinet.

Johnny thought the instrument was beautiful. Full of boyish enthusiasm he took it to school. His music teacher gasped when Johnny opened the case. . . .

Progress was rather slow. Johnny seemed to get so tired blowing his instrument. He wondered why his teacher needed to look up so many fingerings for him. Soon he discoverd that his clarinet was not like the instruments the other children owned. They teased him about the unusual clarinet that he brought to class. It never was quite in tune with theirs. Johnny didn't continue to play for long.

More Casualities

Across the street from Johnny lived Sara Smith. The teacher recommended a flute for her. Her parents also visited the music store and learned that the best flutes are quite expensive. The cost was far too much they thought; so they consulted a

---

[2]James W. Robbins, "All That Glitters Is Not Gold," *The Instrumentalist*, XII, 6, (February, 1958), 33.

mail order catalog. Sure enough, the "Wish-Book" listed flutes, and they cost much less.

The description said that these were "the very best" and that they were made "by a famous European manufacturer." Off the order was sent, and in a few days, back came the flute in a genuine simulated leather case. As the days went by, Sara seemed to be slower in learning than the other girls. She said that her flute was hard to blow, but her parents were convinced that she was just not working hard enough. Turning her over Daddy's knee did not seem to improve things. At last flute lessons were given up, and the flute was in its case to stay.

In the next block lived Tommy. He, too, wanted to play an instrument. Father had played the trombone years ago, and had one up in the attic. The old-timer was brought down, cleaned up, and given to Tommy who had wanted a saxophone. "But we have the trombone already. If you really want to play, you can start on this." Of course, Tommy was a bit short in the arms. He could reach position four on the slide. This made his trombone playing a bit erratic, but then he would grow as the years passed. Unfortunately, he lost interest before his arms grew to the necessary length.

Not Typical Cases?

Perhaps you think that Tommy, Sara, and Johnny are not typical cases. Their names have been invented, but they are quite real. . . . . Many children start lessons on poor instruments, and then become so discouraged that they quit music rather than continue the agony . . . . A fine player (cannot) develop to capacity on a poor instrument.

All flutes, cornets, clarinets are NOT the same. The qualities that make for ease of playing, quality of tone, smoothness of performance, and success of the student are not seen easily by the inexperienced eye. To change the old maxim, all that glitters is not *useful*. A music instrument is intended to produce beautiful music. The cheapest instrument will have a glittering plating of gold or silver, which will wear off in time. And some of the very best instruments may not look much different from the very worst.

Why should anyone expect that a child just starting lessons can use an instrument on which even a professional cannot play well?

Getting the Best

It is (our) hope that parents buying instruments for their children might follow the practice of seeking expert help in this serious matter. The school music teacher is always willing to assist. The following suggestions may also be of use:

1. Get help in the selection of an instrument for your child. A child who could not get a small "beep" on a French horn might make a wonderful oboe player. The school music teacher will be glad to discuss the possibilities or will recommend an expert in this field of diagnosis.
2. Rent a fine instrument for a trial period. Most music stores will rent top quality instruments, just as they will the less expensive ones. If you rent, everyone can tell how Johnny makes out before the instrument is purchased.
3. Buy from a reputable local dealer. If something is wrong about the instrument, he will make it right. Instruments bought from the pawn shop or the mail order catalog may need expensive overhauling which would be at the expense of the buyer, or worse yet, they may be incapable of repair.
4. Buy the very best instrument you can afford. This is not buying frills, engravings on the bell of the horn, and useless luxury in the case. This is buying beauty of tone, quality of production, ease of playing, and success for your child.

One parent remarked to me about this last point just a few months ago. He was ordering a fine instrument for his child and was having me check the order. He said that another of his children had once played the piano. They had an old piano, out of tune, poor key action, and all the other ills of such instruments. The child didn't want to practice. Progress was slow, and at last lessons were stopped. At the time, he thought his child unmusical. Now he told me that he decided that while the family had saved money by keeping the poor piano, they had *lost music* for one child. They had resolved not to make the same mistake with their flute player, even tho it might involve several hundred dollars.

WOOD VERSUS PLASTIC

There is almost always a question about wood versus plastic clarinets. The answer that can be given is: There is no question that superior quality wood clarinets are usually well made and are entirely satisfactory from a musical standpoint. However, their price is often prohibitive for school use because of the high cost of prime Grenadilla and the waste in manufacturing due to cracking and splitting.

Of even greater importance is the cost of upkeep—especially when a wood clarinet receives *improper* care. All wood clarinets, regardless of price, are subject to shrinking, cracking and warping under changing climatic conditions and temperatures and must be handled with extreme care at all times.

Cheap, poorly made, wood clarinets are false economy. Many of these are made in foreign countries by child and other unskilled labor, and of inferior materials. Mechanisms are clumsily made and assembled, with the result that the instruments get out of adjustment within a short time and repairs are often difficult and costly.

Ebonite, which is hard rubber, has been used, with varying degree of success, for many years as a more stable substitute for wood in lower priced clarinets.

While less susceptible to temperature and climatic changes than wood, ebonite is somewhat brittle and is subject to breaking, especially when assembling and taking apart.

Clarinets made of ordinary commercial plastics have the same general characteristics and weaknesses as ebonite clarinets. Certain types of rolled, laminated plastics have many basic advantages over ebonite but unfortunately the cost of this material and working it has, so far, prohibited its use for lower priced clarinets.[3]

---

[3]*Clarinet Dollars and Sense.* Hyde Park, Boston: The Cundy Bettoney Co., p. 1.

When looking at a brass instrument its quality can somewhat be determined by:

1. The material from which it is constructed should not be so thin that it can be easily bent.
2. The lacquer should be smooth and free of bumps and ripples.
3. All slides must move but not so easily as to allow air leakage.
   a. Most valved brass have at least four slides—a main tuning slide and one for each valve.
4. The valves must move freely—neither too stiff nor bounce too freely when released after being depressed.
5. A poorly made instrument, or a very old one will probably leak air around the valves. This can be checked by:
   a. Pulling out the valve slide quickly without depressing the valve.
      (1) If the valves are air tight there will be a "pop."
      (2) If there is no "pop" it means that air is leaking from the valves around the casings into the valve slides. This will make the instrument blow hard. It will also mean that the playing of both high and low notes will be very difficult if not impossible.

MOUTHPIECES

The mouthpiece on an instrument is its most important feature. A good instrument with a poor mouthpiece is much worse than a poor instrument with a good mouthpiece. On good instruments, the mouthpiece is designed to fit the bore of that particular instrument so it is not wise to change a mouthpiece unless absolutely necessary. If the mouthpiece must be changed, purchase an expensive one. Purchase only one of the size and shape recommended by the instrumental teacher. Mouthpiece sizes vary considerably. They come with a great many numbers describing the various dimensions. For ease of playing, a child should have a mouthpiece that fits his particular embouchure. The selection of a mouthpiece can only be done by someone with a knowledge of the various sizes and their relationship to certain types of embouchures and results desired from the instrument.

PARENT AIDS TO CHILD'S SUCCESS

Ways in which parents can help their child profit most by his participation in the instrumental music program include:

1. Help your child acquire and maintain a good wholesome attitude toward school each day. Good manners and co-operation with the group are the results of a wholesome attitude.
2. Uphold the instrumental music instructor should it be necessary to take disciplinary action to improve your child and his activity with the band.
3. If, a parent should remember any misconduct of their own when he was in school, it is not well to discuss it in the presence of children or youth unless you are pointing it out as a mistake your child should avoid.
4. Show an interest in your child's progress as indicated by his grades and the quality of work and achievement displayed during home practice by a compliment when deserved and a word of encouragement from time to time.
5. Realize and help your child to realize that the sole desire of the instrumental music department is to assist him in achieving the highest goal possible.
6. Understand that some students have no interest in the band program, neglect their practice and do not wish to conform to good band class conduct. Therefore, they must be removed from band for their own good and that of the band.
7. Provide a regular time and place for practice and help your child form good work habits by beginning practice promptly at the designated time.
8. Take time to confer with the instrumental teacher when the welfare of your child is involved.
9. Hold decisions on disciplinary problems in abeyance until

the matter is reviewed with the instrument music teacher.

10. The instrumental music teacher is dealing with 350 pupils a day and the perplexities involved in performing music. This of course results in problems. These problems can be solved however, through mutual understanding of student, parent and teacher.

11. Insist that your children conform to the regulations as set forth by the school and the instrumental music department in this policy.

Statistics show that most disciplinary problems have their origin outside the school and discipline problems in the band program are no exception.[4]

Here is an interesting list of items that might be used under certain circumstances:

Parents B#—25 Proven Methods—
For Ruining Your Child's Music Education

1. Buy him the cheapest instrument possible so that he can "look forward" to "earning" a better one.

2. Always point out *all* of his shortcomings; *never* praise. "There's no sense in spoiling him."

3. Always call him for practice when the ball game's going best; call in a loud, demanding voice so his friends will feel sorry for him.

4. Insist he practice a certain time each day without exception. Lay down the law. "Either you practice when I say, or you quit!"

5. Insist he practice the most uninteresting music the longest. "You can't learn to play an instrument by playing tunes!"

6. Don't invite other children in to play instruments with your child. They make too much "noise," "kill" too much time, have too much "fun,"—and track in too much dirt!

7. Be sure to tell father at the dinner table how little son has practiced. Then he won't dare leave anything on his plate.

8. Never help him with his practicing. "I just never have the time."

---

[4]Compiled by Orin Bartholomew, "Ways in Which Parents Can Help Their Child to Profit by His Participation in the Instrumental Program." Public Schools, Eunice, New Mexico.

9. Add another hour of practice when he has been naughty, or doesn't mind you.

10. Call loudly from the kitchen or basement each time he makes a mistake. Add a punch line such as, "Was that a sick cat I heard?" or "If you can't do better than that, better give up."

11. Stop him if he practices anything for fun other than his lesson. "Music is serious!"

12. Threaten, periodically, to stop his lessons, unless: (a) he practices much more, (b) he plays better than so-and-so, (c) he takes better care of his instrument, (d) he makes better grades, (e) he makes his bed each morning, (f) he treats his parents with more respect.

13. Insist on *perfection* in everything connected with his music. 100% or it's no good. "He'll appreciate this when he grows up."

14. Don't let him play for his friends or anybody else until he can *really* play his instrument. After two or three years he'll be able to "surprise" them.

15. Take him unawares the first time you want him to play for someone and ask him in front of everybody to play "something." If he refuses, *insist* that he play; if he still refuses, announce that he's through with music. By all means, don't help him select and work up a number which he can play for company.

16. Don't take him to a concert until he's old enough, and don't take him unless he can play well enough to "appreciate" it.

17. Insist that he take private lessons from the strictest, driest teacher in town.

18. Be sure to point out his shortcomings often, especially in front of teacher or fellow students. "It will make a better impression then."

19. Rest your nerves after a hard day's work by telling him not to practice where you can hear him. "Take that thing down to the basement. Don't I deserve a little peace and quiet?"

20. Insist that he can't take band or orchestra unless his grades improve in his academic subjects. "Band is just play anyhow."

21. Insist that he take Latin in high school instead of band or orchestra. "After all, Latin is required for college entrance!"
22. Don't pay attention to his music making; you don't care whether he practices or not.
23. Use music as a wedge for getting other things done; e.g., if he doesn't wash the dishes every night, threaten to cut off his lessons.
24. Don't buy him a good instrument until he plays "real well." "No sense wasting money!"
25. With some parents, the real secret is to nag effectively and regularly. Others manage to ruin their child's music making by disregarding it almost completely. "If my child likes it, O.K. If not, O.K." Strangely enough, the over-ambitious parent succeeds with amazing consistency!

NOTE: It is not necessary to apply all 25. Usually one or two will do the job.[5]

CONTINUED REPORTING TO PARENTS

Once the beginning band is under way, parent contact should be continued. This is done by reporting to parents at regular intervals. Though most schools will allow the instrumental teacher to enter a grade for band on the regular report card, it is desirable to transfer to parents more information than just one letter or number grade. Therefore it behoves the instrumental department to establish its one separate reporting system. Illustrations 5-8 through 5-10 are some examples of just such reporting devices.

Illustration 5-8[6] is a rather simple, mimeographed, single sheet type report that covers a wide range of items. Illustrations 5-9 and 5-10 are printed cards that do give a very official look to the report.

[5]"Parents B# - 25 Proven Methods for Ruining Your Child's Music Education," *The Instrumentalist*, XIX, 4, (November, 1964), 58.

[6]Emil A. Holz and Roger E. Jacobi, *Teaching Band Instruments to Beginners.* Englewood Cliffs, N.J.: Prentice-Hall, Inc., 1966, p. 79.

ILLUSTRATION 5-8

Elementary Instrumental Music Report

NAME _____ SEMESTER, 19 _____

SCHOOL _____ CLASSROOM TEACHER _____

GRADE _____ CLASS: Beginning _____, Advanced _____

MUSICIANSHIP

The check in the first line of squares indicates the student's performance in relation to the entire class. The check in the second line shows the teacher's estimate of the student's ability in music. The check in the third line shows the student's progress in relation to this estimate of his musical ability.

Comparative Performance	Poor	Fair	Average	Good	Superior
	☐	☐	☐	☐	☐
Estimate of Ability	Poor	Fair	Average	Good	Superior
	☐	☐	☐	☐	☐
Performance vs. Ability	Poor	Fair	Average	Good	Superior
	☐	☐	☐	☐	☐

For each ability used in playing an instrument a letter shows the student's achievement in relation to his own musical capacity: G (good) for achievement at the level of his capacity, F (fair) for achievement somewhat below his capacity, P (poor) for achievement seriously below his capacity.

_____ Tone Quality   _____ Sense of pitch

_____ Knowledge of fingerings   _____ Breath control

_____ Reading of note names   _____ Playing position (posture,
                                                position of hands, instrument,
_____ Sense of rhythm   embouchure)

CITIZENSHIP

The comments below indicate the student's attitudes and cooperation in instrumental music.

_____ Preparation of lessons   _____ Courtesy

_____ Attention in class   _____ Cooperation

_____ Response to instruction   _____ Promptness

_____ Care of equipment   _____ Attendance with instrument, music

A conference with the parent
is always welcomed.   _____
                                   Instrumental Music Teacher

                              Phone: _____

ILLUSTRATION 5-9

"Since music has so much to do with
the molding of character, it is necessary that we teach it to our children."
--Aristotle

Instrumental Music
Report Card

For _____

Date _____

Instructor _____

Daily Average _____

Playing Test _____

Aptitude Test _____

Theory Lessons _____

Total Average _____

PERSONAL COMMENTS:

ILLUSTRATION 5-9—continued

☐ Is making satisfactory progress.

☐ Is making outstanding progress.

☐ Is dependable.

☐ Shows excellent interest in music.

☐ Is ready for a full sized instrument.

☐ Must purchase an instrument by:

☐ It is recommended that a new instrument be purchased.

☐ It is recommended to rent for another semester.

☐ Has already rented beyond the time limit.

☐ Instrument is in need of repair.

☐ Needs: strings, reeds, oil, supplies

☐ Insists on continuing poor playing habits.

☐ Has ability but needs reminding by parents.

☐ Is not practicing enough at home.

☐ Refuses to take instrument home to practice.

☐ Does not realize that without practice one cannot learn.

☐ Cannot tell when playing out of tune.

☐ Is rarely prepared for lessons.

☐ Misses lesson, class.

☐ Shows little desire to learn instrument.

☐ Refuses to bring own instrument to school.

☐ Is tardy to lesson or class.

☐ Cannot remember instructions.

☐ Forgets lesson, instrument, book.

☐ Does not comprehend instructions.

☐ Lacks ability to concentrate.

☐ Should take private lessons due to advanced ability.

☐ Is recommended for further study in the band or orchestra.

☐ Is not recommended for further instrumental study.

☐ Is recommended to continue only under more careful supervision of parents.

☐ Limited musical ability prohibits further progress.

ILLUSTRATION 5-10

PROGRESS REPORT IN INSTRUMENTAL MUSIC
Eunice, New Mexico

This is an effort on the part of the Instrumental Music Department to give you parents a more complete and understandable picture of the progress your child has attained on his chosen instrument. The letter grade can be better understood in terms of progress toward successfully playing his instrument if you follow the check marks and become familiar with the information that they represent. Pupils are not graded by comparison, one to another, but on the manner in which they develop their individual ability to perform on their chosen instrument.

V -- Work Needed Here   VV -- Much Work Needed Here   VVV -- Very Poor, Much Work Needed

A. SUPERIOR. This grade is reserved for the pupil that can play their parts well, and that show evidence of practicing.

B. GOOD. This grade indicates that the pupil plays his part well and does some practicing.

C. AVERAGE. This pupil experiences trouble at times in playing his part because he cannot read the music and cannot finger the notes properly. He probably needs parental help in planning his practice time and in being encouraged to improve himself and his playing.

D. LOW C. This grade is given to pupils that do very poorly at playing, but who may be capable of doing average, good, or superior work. These pupils tend to slow the band's progress to better performance and learning more music because of the extra time they must be given because of their own attention to their practice habits.

PARENTS SIGNATURE:

1................................... 3...................................

2................................... 4...................................

ILLUSTRATION 5-10—continued

STUDENT _____ CLASS _____

	1st 9 Weeks	2nd 9 Weeks	3rd 9 Weeks	4th 9 Weeks
TO IMPROVE TONE:				
Practice in front of a mirror and watch the EMBOUCHURE carefully. (Mouthing the instrument)				
Correct breathing and control of tone.				
TO IMPROVE TECHNIQUE:				
Learn to count and feel the basic beat. Music is build on rhythm.				
Correct improper tongue action.				
Study rhythm patterns and exercises.				
Learn regular and optional fingering.				
TO IMPROVE ATTENTION AND COOPERATION IN CLASSROOM WORK:				
Come with instrument always clean and in repair				
Give close attention to the director and his instructions.				
Pupils use of opportunities available thru the school for a musical education.				
The study habits being developed can help lead to more successful work in all classes in High School				
BAND GRADE				

There is another reporting device that can be used separately or in conjunction with these—*The Watkins-Farnum Performance Scale* (Illustration 5-11). This is the most concrete grading device published. The *Performance Scale* is published in two parts: a Student Testing Book and Scoring Sheets. The scoring sheets make excellent, perhaps the best, reporting devices that can be sent home to parents.

ESTABLISHING A STANDARD

Every subject in the school curriculum, from physical education (in some cases) to spelling and history, has an established standard. This standard, to be sure, may only be established through the use of a particular book for the subject for a given year. The instrumental music department also establishes such a standard by selecting a particular book for each year of training. The social studies teacher further established a standard through testing the children on the material covered in the book used. We have suggested the establishment of a standard through the giving of the *Watkins-Farnum Performance Scale* and the giving of written tests (this is rarely done in instrumental music mostly because it is time consuming). Another method for setting up a standard is through the establishment of a test for each semester of instruction.

Some of the reasons this should be done include:

1. If one should have to justify the program to an administrator there will be concrete evidence that the children are not just blowing for the fun of it. They are really learning something. There is a graduated series of instructional periods, perhaps not week by week but at least semester by semester.
2. It gives the teacher direction. One of the best ways for finding out if the teaching is being successful is through the establishment of some type of uniform testing procedures.
3. If the teacher is really consciencious, he will be interested in making his teaching more effective over the years. The

ILLUSTRATION 5-11

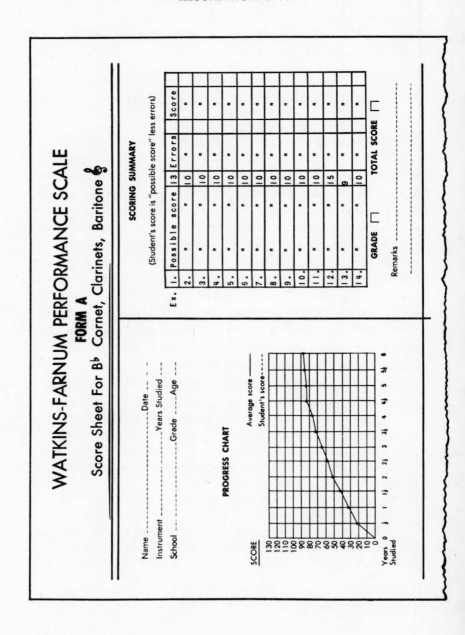

ILLUSTRATION 5-11—continued

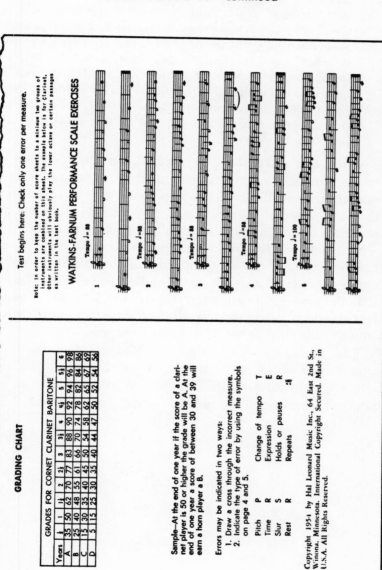

establishment of a standard gives him something to look at and say, hopefully, "That standard I set three years ago seems too easy now? I think I should raise it a little."

4. The most important point for establishing a standard is so that the instrumental music department can give grades to the children in the program. Though it is true that attendance, discipline, and all the other things are important to a successful band, a child in the history class is passed or failed upon his knowledge of history. A child in an English class is passed with an A+ because of his knowledge of English, not because he comes to class every day, has his books, pencil, pen and paper and does not disturb the class by his presence.

When first establishing a standard, one may simply look through the method books being used and make up a test out of that material. Illustration 5-12 is an example of one such test that is quite simple to administer. This test has been used for a number of years in the Utica Public Schools, Utica, New York.

So that all will be aware of its requirements, Illustrations 5-12 and 5-13 would be mimeographed and passed out to the fifth graders about a month before the end of the semester. To facilitate the grading of such a test, Illustration 5-14 would be used by the person giving the test. Illustration 5-15 would be an example of the rhythm for sight reading purposes.

The *Kwalwasser-Rush Test of Musical Accomplishment* would make an excellent testing device. This could be given almost every year. After the first year, one could determine what range of scores would be used for giving various grades.

ILLUSTRATION 5-12

Technical Accomplishments

Pupils should be able—

1. to demonstrate proper playing position and holding of the instrument
2. to assemble and give proper care of the instrument
3. to produce an even tone and demonstrate correct embouchure
4. to play in the meter signatures of 2/4 3/4 4/4
5. to use the foot beat correctly
6. to perform the following scales from memory:
    Treble clef instruments—C, G, F, Bb, chromatic scale one octave
    Bass clef instruments—F, Bb, Eb, chromatic scale one octave
7. to perform a majority of the more elementary rhythmic patterns
8. to perform correctly tonguing techniques, for the required music played
9. to play musically two elementary solos
10. to sight read music selected by the examiner

Theoretical Accomplishments

Pupils should be able—

1. to read the names of the notes rapidly
2. to be able to spell the names of the notes in the scales memorized
3. to recognize and name the major key signatures of the scales learned
4. to know the meaning of about fifteen of the common musical terms and notations used in playing
5. to recognize and give the number of beats in each rhythm studied.

ILLUSTRATION 5-13

1. p—piano—soft
2. pp—pianissimo—very soft
3. mp—mezzo-piano—medium soft
4. cresc. (sign) crescendo - increasing in volume
5. dim. (sign) diminuendo - decreasing in volume
6. f—forte—loud
7. ff—fortissimo—very loud
8. mf—mezzo-forte—medium loud
9. slur—A curved line placed above or below a group of notes to indicate that they are to be played with one breath, and without the use of the tongue.
10. staccato—detached
11. rit.—ritardando—gradually slowing the speed
12. D.C. al Fine—Da Capo—from the beginning al Fine— to the end (a repetition of the piece from the beginning
13. accent mark (a sidewards V) the stress of one tone over the others
14. andante—very moderate speed (to walk)
15. allegro—quick, cheerful
16. moderato—in moderate speed—between andante and allegro
17. hold sign—fermata—means to pause
18. key signature—the sharps or flats appearing at the beginning of the staff which indicates the key of the composition
19. meter signature—the numbers that appear at the beginning of the staff
20. meaning of the upper number—number of counts per measure
21. meaning of the lower number—kind of a note that receives one beat

ILLUSTRATION 5-14

Student's Name _____ School _____

1. Assemble the instrument   ‾‾‾‾

2. Give proper care of the instrument   ‾‾‾‾

3. Scales
   a. Give key for: (1) no # & no b's   ‾‾‾‾
                    (2) one #   ‾‾‾‾
                    (3) one b   ‾‾‾‾
                    (4) two b's   ‾‾‾‾

   b. Spell: (1) C D E F G A B C   ‾‾‾‾
             (2) G A B C D E F# G   ‾‾‾‾
             (3) F G A Bb C D E F   ‾‾‾‾
             (4) Bb C D Eb F G A Bb   ‾‾‾‾

   c. Play: (1) C D E F G A B C   ‾‾‾‾
             (2) G A B C D E F# G   ‾‾‾‾
             (3) F G A Bb C D E F   ‾‾‾‾
             (4) Bb C D Eb F G A Bb   ‾‾‾‾   ‾‾‾‾

4. Play examples of (1) 2/4   ‾‾‾‾
                    (2) 3/4   ‾‾‾‾
                    (3) 4/4   ‾‾‾‾
                    (4) use of the foot beat ‾‾‾‾   ‾‾‾‾

5. Solos: Solo No. 1   Solo No. 2

   a. reading letter names   ‾‾‾‾   ‾‾‾‾
   b. instrument position   ‾‾‾‾   ‾‾‾‾
   c. posture   ‾‾‾‾   ‾‾‾‾
   d. correct embouchure   ‾‾‾‾   ‾‾‾‾
   e. use of foot beat   ‾‾‾‾   ‾‾‾‾
   f. articulation   ‾‾‾‾   ‾‾‾‾   ‾‾‾‾

6. Terminology   ‾‾‾‾

ACCUMULATIVE GRADE _____

(Note -- the lines following each item above is for recording a grade)

ILLUSTRATION 5-15

Typical rhythms that should be played by a first-year student.

6

Strengthening the Elementary Band in the Sixth Grade

The sixth grade program is founded upon the same items as the fifth grade except the children are given additional information to further deepen their understandings of the problems involved in playing their instruments and to increase their musical understandings and technical facility. Their musical understanding will particularly be increased by an ever widening musical vocabulary.

The program is divided as was the fifth grade into class lessons, technic class and band rehearsal. The lessons will involve an increased look, in depth, into solo materials and further technical advancement. The technic class will emphasize the internal workings of band music by using the class as a periodic sectional rehearsal. Through this, the children playing the inner parts can come to understand the very important contribution they make to the whole. Through varied band compositions, there will be an introduction to the different styles in music. The performance of music of greater character is now made possible by increased technical facility. More attention can now be paid to such topics as balance, phrasing, interpretation, etc.

CLASS LESSONS

After a few lessons with a class of young pupils, the teacher will soon discover varying degrees of aptitude. The progress of the more talented pupils should not be retarded, even if the personnel of the class remains the same. Supplementary material should be given to pupils when they show more ability. Following a term of class work the teacher will need in some cases to reclassify the groups to give greater advantage to the slow and fast pupils.

Private lessons are the obvious answer to the problem of the child who is advancing at a faster rate than his fellow classmates. The private lesson, though an easy solution to the problem, does create a real problem when one tries to make room for it in the program. When is this child to be given his lesson? On school time? If it is on school time, how long should the lesson last? If it is to last thirty minutes, and anything shorter would be of little value, is it not unfair to the children who are in classes of five or six persons? Perhaps the biggest question would be, how is it decided which child should take private lessons? Once a few in the school are given private lessons on school time it is possible to conceive that every parent will want their child to study privately also. The parents of the slower children might even suggest that more progress would be made by their child if he were given private lessons.

Many schools make use of the music rooms after school for the giving of private lessons to those who wish to study. In most cases the parents pay for these lessons directly to the teacher. It may be necessary to justify why a teacher should charge for these lessons especially since he will be using school facilities (heat and light particularly). The many hours spent after the school day closes, is usually sufficient explanation. This is a highly specialized form of instruction that the general taxpayer cannot be expected to supply. Those desiring this type instruction should pay for the service directly. The teachers are allowed use of the facilities because, were it not for their employment on a regular basis by the school for class lessons and band, this service would not be available to anyone.

This is more of a problem in the junior and senior high school. By the sixth grade, under normal circumstances the assignment of supplementary materials and through solo playing the above average child can find sufficient challenge to keep him interested.

KEEPING THEM PRACTICING

Continued use of the practice reports aid in keeping the children practicing at home. There are, however, a few other things that can be done. Two different types of charts can be posted in a central location for recording the amount of practice time or the completion of lessons exercises.

THE PRACTICE CHART

The practice chart can be utilized two different ways: individually or as a group item. Illustration 6-1 would be for entering individual names. The squares across the chart would contain a representation of whatever amount of time the teacher may wish to show. In the illustration shown, each square represents two hours. By consulting the chart one can see that Anthony Dee has practiced 21 hours thus far this semester while Richard Webern has put in but 10 hours.

Illustration 6-2 would bring into play group competition. At each lesson one member of the class would collect the practice cards, add them up and enter them onto the chart. Because the classes are made up of five or six individuals, each square on the chart might represent 10 hours. If most classes have six players, in those having just five an equalization might be arrived at by counting the lowest amount of practice for the week twice.

EXERCISE CHART

This too can be individual or group. In this case the exercise that had been successfully completed could be marked off on the chart. If each exercise in the lesson book is numbered, this makes for ease of keeping the chart. If there are just page numbers or lesson numbers these could be used or each line could be numbered for charting purposes. When making up the charts, various colored markers could be used to make them attractive looking.

INDIVIDUAL PRACTICE GRAPH

A score board is set up in the manner of a graph, on regular graph paper. The student then establishes what is going to be termed a mistake. During his practice, he jots down the number of mistakes in each exercise, then accumulates them at the end of the practice period and marks them on the graph.

For a while, the graph will prove to be very irregular in design. When the erratic control on the part of the player is lessened and the player acquires more regular control, the pattern begins to form.

Leonard Smith, who suggested this idea some years ago at a cornet clinic, said that he had known students who, beginning with 150 to 200 mistakes a day, played entire practice sessions with under 50 mistakes inside a three week period.

He further stated that anyone who keeps a graph of his practice in this manner is not going to be satisfied or content with practice for the sake of merely spending time. He is going to have a goal to shoot for. As in golf, he is going to determine what the "par" is for the course; then he is going to break par, then establish a new par for the course and try to break it again.

PRACTICING BECAUSE OF RECITALS

A child's musical experience is only complete in his and his parents' eyes when he can stand on his own two feet and perform music that is pleasurable for himself and for his listeners as well as to participate in the school band. Through the class lesson and the playing of solos, one of these aspirations can be accomplished.

To give emphasis to practice and the learning of solos, the sixth graders could be presented in periodic recitals. Richard and Marjorie Bently presented bi-monthly recitals and described how it functioned and the benefits reaped:

> Bi-monthly student recitals in the . . . schools were our solution to the need for a device to spur music appreciation, aid student progress, and keep interest from flagging.
>
> Recitals were given in the music room at the close of the school day. Parents, teachers and students were invited, and printed programs were provided to add to the importance of the occasion.
>
> Performers learn many important things that can come only from playing in public. Primarily, they have a chance to learn from hearing each other. In addition, they realize the value of poise and stage appearance. They learn how to listen to a performer, what courtesies to expect from an audience, and gain a working knowledge of performer-audience reactions.
>
> Often at recitals we discuss problems related to the use of the different instruments. We sometimes listen to a recording by an outstanding soloist. . . .
>
> After the program each pupil evaluates his performance with us, telling what he thinks he has done successfully and what areas he feels need to be improved. Sometimes this evaluation is aided by use of a tape recorder. The children are more severe critics than we, and are anxious to see how much can be accomplished by the next recital.
>
> We note that large group performances have improved in

ILLUSTRATION 6-1

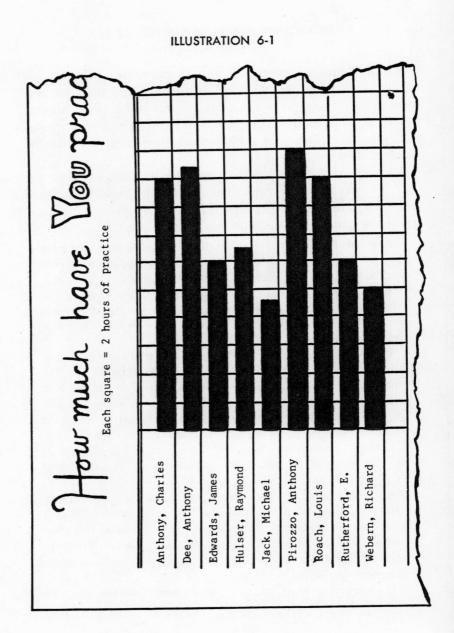

ILLUSTRATION 6-2

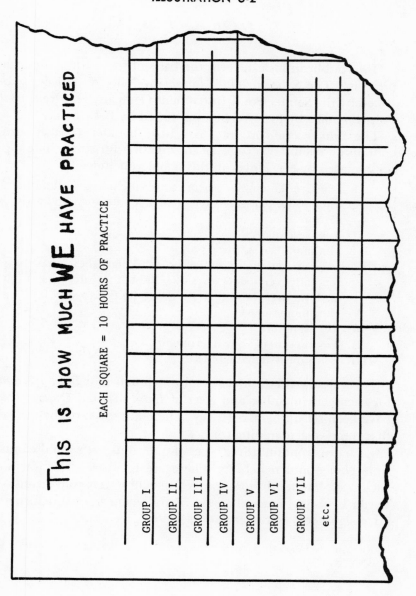

tone quality, phrasing, and dynamic contrast and that general interest in music has increased since the inception of the recitals.[1]

TECHNIC CLASS

Two publications can form the basis of the sixth grade technic class: The *Selmer Band Manual* by Nilo W. Hovey, published by the Selmer Band Instrument Company and *Rehearsal Fundamentals* by Fred Weber, published by Belwin Inc.

The *Selmer Band Manual* is a little booklet (pocket size) containing twenty-two pages of information for study. The topics discussed by Mr. Hovey in this booklet include:

I. Effective ensemble performance—including technique, intonation, phrasing, style, dynamics, balance, and articulation
II. Rehearsal marks
III. Common Terms (over 100)
IV. A comparative list of tempo markings—those that are generally very slow to slow, those that are generally medium and those that are generally fast to very fast.
V. Metronome marks
VI. Key signatures
VII. Taking care of your instrument
VIII. Hints on systematic practice

For a nominal cost, the school can purchase a *Band Manual* for each class member and a set of *Band Manual Quizzes* that have been set up by Mr. Hovey. There are seven of the quizzes that come with a grading form.

Each quiz contains three types of questions: true or false, multiple choice and matching. There are ten basic questions on each test. The tenth question is a matching test containing between 12 and 14 musical terms. By following an outline provided, assignments before each quiz can be given out.

---

[1]Richard and Marjorie Bentley, "Student Recitals." *The Instrumentalist*, VI, 2, (October, 1951), 6.

ILLUSTRATION 6-3

Expression, Style, Articulation and Dynamics

Many times we may hear two players or two bands, each will play the notes and rhythm correctly, play with nice tone and intonation, yet one may sound better and be more exciting and enjoyable to listen to. This is usually the result of expression, style, or musical taste.

On the next six pages the student will become acquainted with some of the fundamental principles of playing musically, in good style or taste, and with expression.

Although we can touch only briefly on each fundamental principle, we hope, with the help of the director, the student will become aware of these things and make a sincere effort to apply them to all of his playing. They are some of the most important things that make the difference between the sound of the amateur player, or band, and the professional.

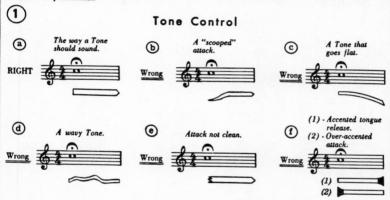

Always strive to produce a tone as indicated in the tone diagram for TONE A. The inability to produce a tone of this type is one of the most common weaknesses of the young musician. While learning to play tones of this type is one of the most difficult things for the young Bandsman to learn to do — it is also one of the most important.

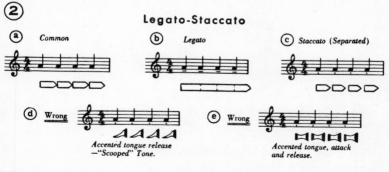

The *Rehearsal Fundamentals* is an all-purpose rehearsal book containing sections on scales, chords and arpeggios, chorales, technic, dynamics, balance and rhythm for developing band musicianship. This makes an excellent companion book to the *Band Manual*. Many discussions in the *Band Manual* can be followed by playing examples for demonstration in the *Rehearsal Fundamentals*. One section in the *Rehearsal Fundamentals* dealing with expression, style, articulation, and dynamics is shown in Illustration 6-3.[2] Later in the book there are equally graphic examples of note emphasis, balance and exercises to have the band become aware of these items in their playing. The final page of the book gives an outline of assignments that could be used. The outline is broken down into fourteen different lessons.

[2]Fred Weber, *Rehearsal Fundamentals*, Rockville Center, L.I., N.Y.: Belwin-Mills Publ. Corp., p. 20.

7

Using the Elementary Band
to Best Advantage

It is conceded that the high school group is more artistically satisfying to the instructor, but there are other satisfactions to be derived from grade school work that are rightly satisfying. The young band can and must be made a complete experience within itself for the student, and must be something more than just a training organization for the advanced groups. The use of the grade school group as a feeder for the high school instrumental group is only secondary in the true educational curriculum.

The musical excellence of some grade school bands bears ample evidence of the high type of musical performance that can be achieved. Even those of us who must start with less have the satisfaction of seeing the young student progress, and we are the recipients of most sincere gratitude from him and his parents. Is there a more appreciative person anywhere than the young student who has profited by our teaching and has been permitted to display his knowledge and skill before his parents and fellow students?

The often discussed question of "Tunes versus Exercises" is not actually controversial, since the common sense approach is the combined method of "Tune *and* Exercises." In guiding the young student, we must always keep in mind the strong motivation derived from the satisfaction of playing a familiar tune or a new tune of a nature familiar to the student. Some technical problems, however, are most efficiently handled through the mechanical approach. The student must receive wise guidance as to time and effort, both technical and artistic, on both tune and exercise.

PARTICIPATION

Planned assembly programs and concerts, or combined concerts with the high school band, provide an outlet for that inherent exhibitionism. The student is frequently reluctant to assume the full responsibility for a solo, but all of them love to "show off" with the group. A planned series of assembly programs and concerts, if judiciously organized, provides progressive and definite objectives toward which the student may be guided. The objective of technical and musical artistry is sufficient motivation for the mature student, but is not grasped by the grade school musician. Therefore, the more immediate objective of displaying real accomplishments to parents and friends becomes the strongest and most practical motivating force to the grade school student.

Competition within the group is another method of stimulation that is very effective and may be carried out through a challenge system, or scheduled try-outs. The most effective system is a combination of spontaneous challenges plus scheduled tryouts which bring the spotlight to bear on the loafer who is content to sit at the end of the section.[1]

TRYOUTS AND CHALLENGES

The *Watkins-Farnum Performance Scale* makes an excellent vehicle for determining chair positions in the band. After each

---

[1]Willard L. Myer, "The Grade School Instrumentalist Not Just Feeders." The Instrumentalist, III, 1, (Sept-Oct., 1948), 8.

child has been given this, the papers are merely placed in order of the highest score first and the positions are thus determined.

Because challenges normally are used for seating the children once the band is under way, it is usually the procedure to have the children play band music for these. Though the *Watkins-Farnum Performance Scale* is of no value in this, concept of grading makes for accuracy in determining the outcome of the challenges.

Determining a student's score on a section in the band music could be as follows:

1. Two copies of the music to be played should be provided. One for the performer and one for the person doing the grading. More than one person could do the grading thus resulting in a more accurate final figure. In this case one copy of the score must be given to each person doing the grading.

2. As the student plays, letters corresponding to the errors made are marked on the score. "A" for articulation errors, "D" for dynamics, "R" for rhythmic, "P" for pitch (a sharp or a flat is placed over notes played in the wrong key) and "T" for tempo. The "T" is placed in the measure where the change was first noticeable. If on the second playing the tempo is still noticeably changed a "T" is marked for every measure.

3. Upon completion of the selection only one error is counted for one measure. If three errors occur in one measure, only one is counted. The total number of measures played is divided into the number of errors and an accurate score is thus arrived at.

If the scoring is very close, the teacher may desire to count more than one error per measure. In this case if the composition is in 4/4 it is conceivable that five or six errors can be counted for a single measure. This then instantly makes the grading of a higher standard without changing the rules. In figuring the score in this manner, the total number of measures played would have to be multiplied by four and then divided into the number of errors.

With this method students can very easily be lined up numerically for tryouts or challenges if the arithmetic is carried out to four or five decimal points. This method does not take into consideration such points as intonation, control, tone, etc. If these items are also to be considered a form like Illustration 7-1 could be used.

ILLUSTRATION 7-1

NAME _____ DATE _____

Composition(s) performed

	excellent A - 4.0	very good B - 3.0	good C - 2.0	fair D - 1.0	poor F - .0
embouchure					
tone					
intonation					
technic					
articulation					
rhythm					
style					
phrasing					
GRADE _____					

PLAYING: number of measures _____

          meter signature   _____

          number of errors   _____

SCORE -------------------- _____

         COMPOSITE score/grade _____

GIVING A GRADE

When giving a grade for embouchure, tone, intonation, technic, articulation, style and phrasing, plus and minus signs may be used so the final scores will have a wider spread. The grade comparison charts (Illustrations 7-2 and 7-3) are for translating the plus and minus into numbers or the "four-point" system. The charts are based upon the usual percentage system with 64 or 74 as failure.

ILLUSTRATION 7-2

with 64 as failure	
A+ = 100 or 4.0	
A = 99 or 3.9	C = 81 or 1.6
A = 98 or 3.6 (3.64)	C = 80 or 1.5
A− = 97 or 3.5 (3.48)	C = 79 or 1.4
A− = 96 or 3.3 (3.32)	C− = 78 or 1.3
A− = 95 or 3.2 (3.16)	C− = 77 or 1.2
B+ = 94 or 3.0	C− = 76 or 1.1
B+ = 93 or 2.9 (2.88)	D+ = 75 or 1.0
B+ = 92 or 2.8 (2.77)	D+ = 74 or 0.9
B = 91 or 2.7 (2.66)	D+ = 73 or 0.8
B = 90 or 2.6 (2.55)	D+ = 72 or 0.7
B = 89 or 2.4 (2.44)	D = 71 or 0.6
B− = 88 or 2.3 (2.33)	D = 70 or 0.5
B− = 87 or 2.2 (2.22)	D = 69 or 0.4
B− = 86 or 2.1 (2.11)	D− = 68 or 0.3
C+ = 85 or 2.0	D− = 67 or 0.2
C+ = 84 or 1.9	D− = 66 or 0.1
C+ = 83 or 1.8	D− = 65 or 0.05
C = 82 or 1.7	F = 64 or 0.0

Because of youthful enthusiasm over "challenging," the band director could get into a real bind. Children have been known to challenge constantly and re-challenge and challenge again. Though this enthusiasm must not be thwarted, it can be very time consuming and not really end up in being of value to those involved. A set of rules governing challenges makes for clarity of purpose and organizational procedures. Some suggested rules for governing challenges are as follows:

The opportunity to challenge is given so that the child who may have improved greatly during the semester does not have to wait for the next semester's tryouts to gain a higher chair in the section.

ILLUSTRATION 7-3

with 74 as failure

A+ = 100 or 4.0			
A = 99 or 3.8		C = 86 or 1.7	
A = 98 or 3.6 (.364)		C = 85 or 1.6 (1.56)	
A = 97 or 3.5 (3.48)		C = 84 or 1.4 (1.42)	
A− = 96 or 3.3 (3.32)		C− = 83 or 1.3 (1.28)	
A− = 95 or 3.3 (3.16)		C− = 82 or 1.1 (1.14)	
B+ = 94 or 3.0		D+ = 81 or 1.0	
B+ = 93 or 2.8		D+ = 80 or 0.8	
B = 92 or 2.6 (2.64)		D = 79 or 0.6 (0.64)	
B = 91 or 2.5 (2.48)		D = 78 or 0.5 (0.48)	
B− = 90 or 2.3 (2.32)		D = 77 or 0.3 (0.32)	
B− = 89 or 2.2 (2.16)		D− = 76 or 0.2 (0.16)	
C+ = 88 or 2.0		D− = 75 or 0.1	
C+ = 87 or 1.8 (1.84)		F = 74 or 0.0	

1. The challenger must notify the challengee at least four days in advance of when he desires to challenge and state what material he will challenge upon. The challenger selects the music.
2. No challenging shall be allowed three weeks preceding a concert if the results may mean a change in musical parts for either party involved in the challenge.
3. No challenging, under any circumstances shall be allowed one week preceding a concert.
4. Material to be used for the challenge must be that currently in use by the organization. If the challenger is to move up to another part he must pick material from that higher part.
5. The challenger plays first.
6. The person challenging must win by a substantial margin, i.e., one tenth of a percent or more. If it is closer than one tenth, further playing must proceed. The person in charge than selects some sight-reading materials.
7. If the playing is still not conclusive, the challenger may re-challenge one week later.
8. If the challenger loses, he must wait four weeks before challenging again.
9. If the challengee loses, he must wait two weeks before re-challenging.
10. The lowest person in the section is allowed to challenge first. If the challengee loses, he forfeits his right to challenge for the next chair up.
11. If the lowest challenger wins, and the challengee has previously stated that he was to challenge the next chair higher, then the winner of the first challenge has the right to challenge the next above his defeated challengee immediately. The challenger must use the music the challengee has previously decided to use.
12. If the challengee should fail to appear at the appointed time, regardless of the reasons, the challenger moves up.
13. If the challenger should fail to appear at the appointed time, regardless of the reasons, it shall be treated as though the challengee had won.
14. No one may refuse a challenge. A person refusing a challenge concedes his seat to the challenger.

THE BAND REHEARSAL

Mr. Joseph Contino has set down some important considerations for conducting band rehearsals. Mr. Contino writes:

The apparent apathy of players in many musical organizations can be attributed to a loosely conducted rehearsal. If such is the case, much of the problem of gaining and keeping interest high can be solved by making the rehearsal a thoroughly business-like and well-disciplined affair. . . .

Starting on Time

Punctuality is of prime importance. This can be best established by starting on time, calling attention to the fact that the specified hour is at hand. It is necessary, of course, to have the physical set-up (stands, chairs, music, etc.) prepared beforehand. A beginning routine of unison scales or chord progressions, following the conductor in various speeds, dynamics, legato, staccato, etc., is valuable for the following reason: (1) it enables the rehearsal to start on time with disregard for the occasional tardiness of key players, (2) it gives the players a chance to review all scales and to listen carefully, and (3) it gives the players a satisfying experience in trying to match the conductor's gestures.

Podium

A podium at least twelve inches high is a must for two reasons: (1) it enables the players to see the conductor better, and (2) it encourages the association between the conductor's presence there and an attitude of "business." The conductor should be on it only when he is actually conducting or discussing the music being played. When speaking about administrative matters, or between numbers, he should step off. The podium, then, should come to be associated with attentiveness and musical matters. . . .

Timing

Conducting demands, and efficiency requires, that a certain timing be adopted whereby the players find their places, come to playing position, and begin playing. After instructions have been given and an interval of about five seconds allowed for the players to find the place (unless many measures are to be counted), the baton (or hands) should be raised, followed by not more than a three second interval for the players to come to a playing position. The times indicated are arbitrary, the point being that there should be little or no delay in allowing for the straggler or in repeating instructions. This "hurry up" process tends to short-circuit talking as well. The conductor should not talk after the baton has gone up, except possibly to give a verbal cue. If he remembers something he must say, and this should be kept to an absolute minimum, he should drop his arms to the sides and give a brief apology for having given a premature "ready" sign. A curt "sorry" will suffice. Such an apology will further impress on the players that when the baton is up, playing is to follow immediately.

Absolute Silence

Absolute silence when not playing is an ideal more readily achieved than many directors believe possible. The following rules or a similar set, rigidly adhered to, should prove effective:

1. Stop conducting when you have something genuinely important to offer in interpretation, balance, etc. This stopping should be a positive gesture, such as raising both arms over head, lowering them to the sides. Playing should stop almost immediately.
2. Do not begin talking until all noise (playing or talking) has ceased. It may take one or two rehearsals to impress this procedure on the players and to break previously acquired habits. If noise or talking persists, the following devices in order of preference are effective in eliminating it:

a. Catch the eye of the offender and keep staring until he stops.
b. Stare either at the floor or straight ahead (possibly with arms folded) until all noise stops. A mildy sarcastic "thank you" after all noise subsides may be effective in putting across the idea, if it fits in with your personality.
c. Say "Please!" in a voice loud enough to be heard.
d. Call out the offender's name.
3. Speak in a normal voice, yet loud enough to be heard by every member. An excessively loud voice encourages increasingly louder noise and talking, resulting in both a hoarse voice for the conductor and loose rehearsal discipline for the organization.

Remarks should be directed to as large a part of the organization as feasible, in matters of interpretation and balance it is frequently feasible to suggest how the entire group, or a large part of it, can adapt to the section being corrected. When indicating the interpretation of a passage played by various sections at different points in the music, it is time-saving to give instructions to all the sections involved when the question first arises, rather than to repeat the remarks as the sections come to the passage. Talking by the director should be kept to a minimum. If an explanation or work with an individual or section must be necessarily lengthy, direct your remarks to the entire group explaining as you work what you are doing and why.

Stopping on time is a courtesy to the players. Budgeting rehearsal time, especially towards the end, should result in finishing a piece of music within a minute or two of stopping time. Before being dismissed, players should be thanked and comment made about the rehearsal, such as "good rehearsal," or "you did very well today."

Infrequently, (it is hoped practically never), circumstances require a conductor to sight read a score with simultaneous sight reading by the players. A helpful device in this instance is to discuss the score with the players beforehand, noting (for them and for yourself) key changes, meter changes, fermata, dynamics, etc.

The following practices are additional time-savers and should be considered well worth establishing:

1. Plan rehearsals ahead of time, budgeting the time to be spent on each number.

2. In order of preference, use one of the following methods to announce the numbers to be rehearsed: a) Blackboard (small portable ones are relatively inexpensive) ; b) Mimeograph or ditto the list of numbers and distribute one to each stand; c) Announce two or three numbers at a time instead of the usual one.

3. Correct during the actual playing if possible. If the director cannot be heard or if he cannot explain quickly enough, or should he require the players to mark their music, he should then, of course stop the ensemble.

4. Do not pass out music at rehearsals. If it is found absolutely necessary to do so, let the librarian pass it out while the organization continues to rehearse.

5. Risers are of definite value in that they a) enable the players to see the conductor better; b) let him feel less confined; d) result in a clearer, more definite musical sound heard by more players.

6. Have on hand a dozen or so sharpened pencils ready for distribution to the inevitable few who may have forgotten to bring theirs.

The director should keep uppermost in his mind that the rehearsal is primarily a means for the players to learn the relationship of their parts to the whole. If the director is equipped to show these relationships, he owes it to the players and to himself to be as efficient as possible in the process.[2]

Some items to watch when rehearsing —
And some possible solutions

1. Rhythm

    a. Long notes♩ , ♩., ○ must be held for their full value.

---

[2]Joseph Contino, "Rehearsal Technics." *The Leblanc Bandsman* (date unknown)

(1) For possible solution see the discussion that accompanies Illustrations 3-2 through 3-5.

b. ♩. ♪ Invariably the eighth note is not given full value.

The note following the eighth is usually played too soon.

It may be played more like ♩. ♫♩

(1) A possible solution may be arrived at by beating consecutive eighth notes or feel a tenuto on the eighth note.

c. ♩. ♪ in 4/4 or 2/4 is usually performed more like

♩ ♪ in 6/8.

(1) A solution may be arrived at by beating sixteenths, making the interpretation such that the sixteenth goes with the next note—not the dotted eighth with the sixteenth. Consecutive figures of this sort would

be played as if they were written ♪ ♫. ♫. ♪

or the sixteenth could be treated more like a

long grace note leading to a quarter ♪♩ ♪♩ ♪♩

In some instances a spacing may improve the situation. This may only be done if it is in keeping with the style of the composition. The figure then would

be played more like this: ♩ ♪ ♩ ♪

d. Two equal eighth notes (♫) are often played more

like an eighth and quarter (♪ ♩) in 6/8.

(1) A solution may be to think of the first eighth note

as having a tenuto under it (♫) or by beating

eighth notes.

(a) Some conductors tap on the music stand with their baton, others simply clap their hands.

      (b) Using a metronome with each click represent-
ing an eighth or a sixteenth, if the tempo is
slow enough, would be the best idea if one is
handy and doing it does not interrupt the flow
of the rehearsal.

e. ♪♪♪ are invariably played more like ♪♪♪

    (1) A possible solution may be achieved by having the
erring section play the section as though the triplets

were actually written ♪♪♩ Now compare

that with what was played and what should have
been played.

    (2) Also, beat out consecutive triplets with the clapping
of the hands while the children play.

    (3) Have part of the section play consecutive triplets re-
gardless of the rhythm while some play the rhythm
written.

f. Consecutive eighths or sixteenths (♪♪♪♩ or

♪♪♪♪) are almost always rushed, especially if

they are contained in a rising line.

    (1) The best solution is a metronome set for the eighth
or sixteenth note which ever the rhythm might be.

g. Consecutively articulated sixteenths (♪♪♪♩ ♪♪♪♩)

will invariably be played more like this: ♪♪♪. ♪♪♪.

    (1) A possible solution is to beat the sixteenth with the
clapping hands or better yet, a metronome.

      (a) There may be a real problem here because of a
lack of facility to articulate accurately with
even, reiterated tongue motions. See the discussion on articulation in Chapter II "Outline
for teaching the clarient to beginners."

NOTE: Problems in articulating rapidly do not always lie

with the tongue. Many, many times it centers around the use
of the breath, i.e., it does not maintain a steady, uninterrupted
flow retaining its resiliency against the tongue.

h. The second note of a two note slur (♪♪ or ♪♪)

rising or falling might encounter two difficulties. First,
as with the playing of two equal eighth notes, the first
one may be played too short, getting to the second note
too soon and/or the second note may be chopped off so

the figure is played more like this: ♪♪ ⅞ or ♪♪ ⅞

Sometimes the shortening of the note is desirable for
stylistic purposes but only if it is done intentionally.

2. Attacks
   a. Ragged attacks are caused by indefiniteness of the con-
      ductors preparatory beat and/or the childrens' lack of
      proper preparation.
      (1) A possible solution besides a conductor being sure
          he has the tempo firmly in mind before starting is
          to discuss the phases of making an attack with the
          band members.
          (a) breath
          (b) set the embouchure
          (c) set the tongue
          (d) blow
          (e) release the tone at the time the beat is to start
      NOTE: The word "attack" is a poor one though it is
      universally used. It should be: "release" the sound from
      the instrument or "release" the air from behind the
      tongue.
      (2) Play the first note of a composition or section several
          times as though there were a fermata over it.
          (a) See that every eye is on the conductor and re-
              mains there when the composition is being
              played.

   NOTE: The conductor's eye should also be on the group.
      (3) Refrain from saying "one, two, ready, go" each time

a piece or section is started. This teaches the children not to watch the baton.

3. Entrances after a rest
   a. When an entrance begins at the bar line there usually will be little trouble if the children are taught to count measures of rest. The children down a section can be taught not to rely upon the first chair member by having him on pre-arranged days place his instrument to his mouth too early at times or maybe not play at all at other times.
   b. Entrances are a problem when they come toward the end of the measure and especially if they happen to be an eighth note anacrusis.
      (1) A possible solution is to have the children bring their instruments up to the mouth at the beginning of the measure and count as though they were actually playing consecutive eighth notes before they play.
         (a) The breath must be taken early in the measure and embouchure set at least a full beat before the beat at which they should come in on.
         (b) Drilling the section, i.e., doing it over several times at different speeds—both slower and much faster than at the ultimate speed the composition is to be played at will draw attention to the problem in the minds of the studdents.
4. Balance
   a. The melody must be heard—harmony parts must be softer. Point out the melody by:
      (1) Playing sections of the composition through allowing only those with the melody to play.
         (a) This might be quite a chore if the melody is a series of short motives or in imitation.
      (2) Have the harmony parts play and keep hushing them down to a whisper. Do it too soft a few times.
      (3) A general rule—long notes are soft notes especially if there are moving notes being played by others.
      (4) Dynamic marks are often only general level indicators.

      (a) It may be that a section marked *forte* for a group of instruments may have to be played *piano* in order to properly balance the melody. The opposite may also be true.

  b. Balance chords

    (1) Can you hear the tonic—what instruments are playing it?

    (2) The inner parts are too often not heard at all—just the top and the bottom of the band.

    (3) On seventh chords the dissonances may have to be played a little louder than the rest so it does not sound like a mistake.

    (4) All notes that are accidentals should be played a little louder especially if they change they key or point up the minor in a major section, etc.

    (5) Isolating an important chord and playing it from the bottom up will help the ears of the conductor—and those of the band also.

5. Tempo changes that are not called for in the score are more the conductor's fault than the band's.

  a. Compositions have a tendency to slow down for soft passages and speed up for loud ones.

    (1) Tape record the rehearsal and try to put a metronome on some of the pieces.

    (2) Make the band play a piece like a march with a metronome turned on. A metronome with a light on the top may be necessary unless the band can play soft enough or the metronome's beat could be put through a loud speaker system.

6. Dynamics

  a. Dynamic changes MUST be heard. Too often the band plays at a *mezzo forte* level continuously. Then in a fast piece it plays everything *fortissimo*.

    (1) Practice warm-up scales with eight beats on each note.

      (a) Start *piano* and crescendo to *forte*.

      (b) A few weeks later start *piano* and crescendo to *fortissimo*.

      (c) Then start *pianissimo* and crescendo to *fortissimo*

  (d) Finally, start *pianississimo* and crescendo to fortississimo.
    (1) Be sure to always maintain a good tone—never allow the band to overblow.
 (2) The group must know what to do with the air stream in order to make a crescendo and diminuendo:
  (a) Loud does not mean to blow hard—it means to blow more air through the instrument.
  (b) To play soft does not mean to blow only a little air through the instrument or to blow easy.
    (1) To play loud, blow the air rapidly through the instrument. The air moves very fast.
    (2) To play soft, the air moves slowly through the instrument. It should seem to the players that they are actually blowing harder to play soft because the intensity is greater but the flow of air is slow. It is of greatest importance to keep the intensity of the air high at all times—not just playing loud.
  (c) The apature must change so the pitch remains the same
    (1) When making a crescendo the apature must open ever so slightly
    (2) When making decrescendo the apature must close ever so slightly

SELECTING MUSIC

Beginning in the late 1950's a large number of publishers began putting out a wide variety of compositions that were designed for the elementary band. Such titles as "First Concert Folio," "First Class Band Folio," "First Performance" and "First Division Band" began appearing on the scene. Several companies published individual works in the form of series. Kendor has a large series of works for the very young elementary band under the title: "Playground Series for Elementary Bands." Luverne has a series also for the very young band. Of a slightly more advanced but still very easy nature is the "Red Band Series" by Pro Art, the "Cadet Series for Young Bands" by Kendor, the Belwin "Series for Young Bands," the "Youth Concert Series" by Robbins Music Corporation and the Mills "First Performance Band Series."

Many of these compositions are newly composed by men familiar with the needs of the elementary instrumentalist. A large number are based upon folk melodies that the children know and enjoy playing. Some are taken from great works and settings of hymns.

The music one selects for his group to play must of course be within the abilities of the youngsters. It must not be too easy but if it is too difficult it will be discouraging to all—the conductor and students alike. A composition selected for the group to play must be at a level that would allow them to play it through fairly well at sight. If the composition must be waded through measure by measure at the first playing it will take weeks and even months before it can be played. Children want to play. That is what they are in the band for. The music must be challenging but not disheartening.

1. Select music that is within the range of the group.
   a. A glance through the exercise books being used by the various groups within the band and noting the highest and lowest notes that appear will give a guide as to what ranges would be possible.
2. Select music that is within the rhythmic realms known to the students.
   a. Making note of the various rhythms studied thus far gives a good guide to selecting compositions. Though introducing new rhythms to the children at band rehearsal is not dangerous, why waste the time when the children could be playing things already within their knowledge?

3. Select music that contains the key signatures already learned by the children.

   a. Selecting pieces with sharps and flats that the children have not learned in the class lesson wastes valuable rehearsal time.

4. Meters used should be simple ones, such as 2/4, 3/4 and 4/4; 6/8 if this has appeared in their lessons. Avoid compound meters.

5. Avoid music that features the weaker sections of the band. Music that contains cross-cueing is a helpful device toward assuring a successful presentation of the composition.

6. The music should have some inner-voice interest. All players deserve an occasional chance to play melodic lines.

7. Select pieces that give the percussionists something to do. Those pieces using the various percussion instruments including cymbals, tambourine, bells, tympani (if a set is available) wood blocks, triangle, and maracas make for interest in a performance besides giving all the percussionists a feel of their realm of contribution.

8. Young performers, their fellow classmates, and their parents who will make up the audiences are easily satisfied by novelty and light concert type pieces but the folders should be stocked with a well-balanced variety of music including not only novelties and marches but some music that has stood the test of time.

9. The music should be printed clearly and contain rehearsal letters or numbers.

10. A full score, though rarely provided for elementary band works, is a great aid for rehearsal procedures.

DROP-OUTS

There have been many investigations into the reasons and causes for students dropping out of the instrumental program. Hal Bergen made a comprehensive study of this as a doctoral dissertation that was submitted to the school for advanced graduate study of Michigan State University. Mr. Bergen found that students drop instrumental music because:

1. They are improperly motivated through:
   (a) High pressure tactics
   (b) Influence of friends
   (c) Pressure from parents
2. They are not selected by test methods which will increase their chances of making progress.
3. The music teachers do not establish positive working relationships with the parents of their students.
4. The objectives of music education are not made clear.
5. Of the lack of orientation and co-operation between elementary, junior high, and senior high school.
6. Of the discouraging junior high school practice of transferring instruments.
7. Of the low quality of school-provided musical instruments.
8. Of poor pupil-teacher relations.
9. Of the selection of low motivating music materials.
10. Of poor methods of evaluation.
11. Of lack of recognition in the group.
12. Of unrealistic demands upon their time.
13. Of the influence of others who drop.
14. Of problems of class schedules.
15. Of the necessity or desire to spend their time earning extra money.

Last Grade in Which Drop-Outs Participated

The five schools studied follow the 6-3-3 plan. It is interesting to note the sudden increase in the drop-out rate from the end of the fifth grade to the end of the sixth grade. Increasing tempo of social life and competition from the other activities takes a significant toll again at the end of the eighth grade, culminating in the peak of drop-outs at the close of the ninth grade —35.1 percent.

Position of Drop-Outs in the Organization

The fact that fifty-six or 37.8 percent of the drop-outs had held from fourth to first chairs in the organization may come as a surprise to the reader. This figure, however, is tempered somewhat by the fact that many of them played in small sections such as bass clarinets, viola and French horn, where nearly anyone would find little difficulty in being assigned one of these chairs. The other ninety-two, or 62.2 percent, were toward the end or at the end of the sections. The first figure challenges the validity of the statement that potential drop-outs are in a no talent classification.

The drop-outs averaged three and one-half years of participation in the school music program. Three and one half years—at the close of which almost a third of the respondents expressed the feeling that they could see no use for music in their futures. It was of interest to note that less than half of the drop-outs owned their instruments while 69 percent of the non-drop-outs did own their own instruments.

Mr. Bergen found that the "student did not feel that he was achieving the musical satisfaction that he had hoped for and so dropped his instrument. Mr. Bergen feels that this is not an indictment of music per se, as is evidenced by the fact that a large majority of the drop-outs stated that they still enjoy listening to music, although the quality was not defined. However, it does seem to be an indictment of methods of music education. It is that too much emphasis is placed on routine drill, too much preparation is made for concerts and festivals, that there is too much preoccupation for schedule performances to the neglect of student satisfaction in the performance of good music for its own sake.[3]

REDUCING DROP-OUTS

The heart of the entire instrumental music program resides in the elementary school, and the lifeblood of this heart is *interest*. Music conservatories and professional musicians will stress musicianship, theory, performance, and other important factors, but in the final analysis, all these are secondary to the elemen-

[3] Hal Bergen, "Drop-outs In Instrumental Music." *The Leblanc Bandsman,* March 1960.

tary instrumental music teacher's ability to maintain interest.

The successful teacher projects his thinking in terms of his students. To this end has Norman Ward contributed the following information on "Reducing Elementary School Drop-out Rates."[4]

During the course of a year many grade school instrumental music teachers find that some of their promising students drop out of the program. Unnecessary drop-outs can hurt a program that depends upon continuity for success. A good program perpetuates itself from year to year but a program can only be successful if the children stay in it! What is it about certain schools and their music programs that continually produce top-notch players and outstanding bands and orchestras? What magic do their teachers wield?

Before discussing the undesirable drop-outs, it must be understood that it is normal for a certain percentage of beginners to stop taking lessons. No matter how foolproof our auditions are, a small number of children slip into the program who should not be there. After the first month the alert teacher will know these students and will take them out of the program immediately, since these students, if not dropped, hurt themselves, to say nothing of the program. A school with a good music reputation was found to lose 20% of its original enrollment in this way.

Now let us consider the child with talent who turns in his instrument. Why does he quit? He is musical, finds the instrument easy to play, but he quits. In most cases the reason for this boils down to one key factor: the teacher. Somewhere along the line he has failed to keep the child interested. What kind of program has he offered the child? What is his personal drawing power? We shall examine these two questions.

The Program

A child drops an instrument because he has lost interest. Although this may seem obvious, many teachers do not try to

---

[4]The following (through page 191) is by Norman Ward, "Reducing Elementary School Drop-Out Rates. "*The Instrumentalist*, XVI, 3 (November, 1961), 38.

understand a child's way of thinking and do not offer him a child's rewards. A nine year old child certainly is not thinking of the benefits music will have for him in the future. He is thinking of now. He is thinking of: playing with a band, wearing a uniform, playing for his friends and relatives, receiving good grades, compliments from the teacher, medals, awards, recognition and so forth! *This* is a child's world.

It is not enough for him to take his lesson every week and do no more. He is expected to practice at least thirty minutes each day and so deserves more of a reward.

First it is recommended that the elementary program include:

1. A training band to be formed no later than January of a school year and having at least one rehearsal a week.
2. An advanced band which starts at the beginning of the school year and rehearses at least twice weekly. . . .
3. Ensembles for the better players to be formed by mid-year.

Putting children into groups at the beginning of school is the biggest weapon against drop-outs.

Secondly, it is recommended that the following practices be carried on throughout the year:

1. A talk with a parent of each student in the program at least once a year. Help from the "home-front" is invaluable to the teacher. Many students who were about to quit were brought back into the fold because of the warmhearted talk with a parent. Not only does the teacher learn much about a pupil when he gets the parents-eye-view but the parent is shown by the teacher how to help the child.
2. Performances are necessary to maintain interest. The children need certain goals at which to aim through the year:
   a. Beginners band should perform at the spring concert.
   b. Advanced band needs a few performances a term. Participation at festivals affords much excitement for the children—one more reason to stay in the program. (They love to win medals.)
   c. Outstanding pupils should have a chance to play solos at concerts and festivals at least once a term.
   d. Children should be encouraged to play for their classes.

3. A mark should go in the teacher's record book for each child after each lesson and a grade be entered on the child's report card along with the school grades. In the child's mind this raises the importance of his lessons. Children need tangible recognition. They like being graded.

4. The music selected should be balanced and of higher caliber . . . . An occasional popular number or novelty is recommended but these pieces must be in correct proportion to the others.

The Teacher

The crux of the whole matter is the teacher himself. The program rises or falls with him. He must be well liked, well organized, and know his subject. He must be creative. He must like children, understand them and be able to reach them. When an alert teacher senses a good student is losing interest, he will think of many ways to lure back his interest. A child should look forward to being with his teacher. One grade school band was so strictly regimented that the children actually were afraid to come to rehearsals. The director had many drop-outs the following year and later resigned his post.

One creative director made an unusual offer in fun. He offered a baby alligator to the child who learned a difficult band piece the best by a given time. The idea was a source of great fun for the children. They learned the piece quickly and were tickled pink when the winner was awarded her 8 inch alligator. It is touches like this which keep a child excited about a program.

Below is a list of questions that might be asked of the teacher to determine his "drawing power."

1. Does he spur each pupil on with warranted praise?
2. Does he reward the child who excels?
3. Does the teacher constantly think of new ways to make a lesson interesting? (Have you tried having a long-tone contest for beginning wind players?)

4. Do the quicker students always have a challenge confronting them?

5. When a good student tells the teacher he has decided to turn in his instrument, does the teacher leave it at that or does he dig into the problem and do everything in his power to get the child back? (When all else has failed, try switching instruments.)

6. Has he checked each child's instrument carefully to see if the trouble lies with the instrument?

7. Are band rehearsals controlled yet relaxed? Do they move rapidly keeping everyone involved?

8. Is care taken that newcomers to the band are not given music that is over their heads? This frustration has led to many a tear and some sensitive children might quit. (Simplify tough parts.)

9. Is the director "all business" or does he inject a touch of humor into his lessons and rehearsals?

10. Does the director embarrass some players in front of his friends or

11. Has he developed an atmosphere at rehearsals where a child, when corrected, does not feel scolded or ridiculed?

12. Does he give the children a chance to conduct?

13. Does he encourage student compositions? (One director has a composition contest. The winning pieces are performed at the spring concert.)

14. Does the band have uniforms?

15. Are the children urged to attend upper grade and community concerts?

16. Are the lessons and band rooms cheerful?

17. Is there a bulletin board? Is it informative, and interesting?

18. Does the director have an outing of some kind for his major groups at the end of the year?

The teacher is the key to the success of his program and hence to the decline of unnecessary drop-outs. His personality, his organizational abilities, and his creativeness in sum total determines the degree of success in keeping promising students in the program.

AWARDS

"The average American will work harder for a $5 plaque than a $50 bill—in business, school sports, clubs, hobbies, fund drives, civic work, and music making," says a Dallas, Texas trophy manufacturer.

Awards somehow have become a modern status symbol—along with foreign cars transistor radios, credit cards, wall-to-wall carpeting, and country club membership—but with a difference; even a millionaire does not buy trophies for himself! To carry prestige, an award must be given by a school, club, business, church, athletic league, or other groups or by an individual.

Awards are used by many (band) directors for purposes of motivation; however, they are equally important in providing opportunity for formal recognition of the service given throughout the year by (band) members. One interesting result of awards programs is that the recipient of awards frequently find additional support from parents, many adults tending to see more purpose in instrumental practice and (band) membership once an impressive trophy is brought home for display to family and friends.

TYPES OF AWARDS

A standard award should be given for each successive year of service. . . . These basic awards may be earned by individuals who meet the specific "lettering" requirements set forth by the director at the beginning of the year.

Special awards add "spice" to the program by allowing outstanding students to receive additional recognition. Such awards should be presented last . . . thus allowing tension to mount before announcing, for instance, the top award of the year—Most Outstanding Musician.[5]

The usual types of awards given are school letters for the first year followed by a music pin.

One may also consider the giving of a certificate. If a certificate is given it is well worth the money to have some printed up special for the band and perhaps the band of a particular school. An ordinary music certificate will not really be as impressive as a real, specially printed "Certificate for Valuable Service" to the (school's name) Band. So as this becomes a constant reminder of the child's success, the instrumental budget can well afford to give this award to the child already framed for hanging on the dining room or the living room wall. If it is not framed it may get lost in a dresser drawer.

Who receives the award can be easily determined by keeping records of the students' participation, lessons, grades on tests and deportment. Totaling all these things up and giving awards to those with above average grades is fairly simple to figure. The child with the highest grade gets a special gold certificate for being the *Most Outstanding Musician of the Year.*

[5]Joan Boney, "An Awards Program for Your Orchestra or Band." *The Instrumentalist*, XVIII, 3, (October, 1962), 60.

8

Keeping Records for the Elementary Band

There are five types of records that must be kept by the band director-instrumental teacher:

1. The students' lessons and their week-by-week progress
2. The record of each child's progress from semester to semester
3. The equipment owned by the school
4. The school-owned instruments and who is using them
5. The music owned by the school and its location

WEEK-BY-WEEK STUDENT RECORD

Keeping a record of the students' lessons on a week-by-week basis prevents the teacher from going to class and saying: "Let's all turn to the lesson for today. . . . What page were we on? . . . Now, what was it we were discussing at the end of the period last week?" It also prevents— in the course of the class: "Didn't I ask you to clean out that mouthpiece last week? The record would show the child was told to get the dirt out of that mouthpiece. A child might say: "You didn't tell me that!" (Whatever "that" might have been.) The teacher could say: "I wrote it down in my book when I told you. You want to see what I wrote?" Many children find interesting excuses why they didn't practice, why they forgot their instrument, why they forgot their music, why they forgot when they were supposed to have a lesson, etc. A record of these "excuses" in the teacher's "little black book" means they cannot use them too often and will, if a record is kept be less likely to use any at all.

The most important reason for keeping this record is so the teacher has an accurate record of progress. This record is the greatest aid, perhaps it should be said an indispensable aid to carrying out the curriculum, re-evaluating the curriculum, revising the curriculum and determining its effectiveness.

This week-by-week account could contain:

1. A list of the class members
    a. It could also contain the serial number of their instruments, their homeroom number and their home telephone number
2. The music being studied by the class
3. The page or lesson on which the group is working
4. A place for entering grades the children receive for their lessons
5. If practice cards are issued, a place for the recording of the amount each child has practiced
6. A record of the number of absences
7. A record of each child's attitudes and actions in the class
8. A place for comments that may have been discussed in the class that might need reviewing at the next lesson or can be discussed in the technic class.

The means of keeping this record are really quite simple. There are three forms in which this can be done:

1. a simple notebook
2. an ordinary filing folder
3. a practice record book

It will be found that if one desires to keep an account of the afore mentioned information the ordinary roll book used by classroom teachers will not suffice. They simply do not have sufficient space for recording all the information. The normal type of roll book is set up mostly for recording absences and a few letter or number grades.

USING A NOTEBOOK

If the instrumental teacher has to travel between several schools this record could be kept in a notebook that would slip into his suit coat pocket. Illustration 8-1 is an example of a page that would be in this type notebook. The size used here has pages that measure 3 3/4" by 6 3/4." One could use the 6" by 9 1/2" sized notebook if he desires a little more space.

Illustration 8-1 is what might be considered as the compact form. This form will not allow a recording of a grade for each lesson or the keeping of a record of the child's practice for each week. It would nevertheless keep a record of the more important items especially considering the practice report is in itself a week-by-week record. The dates, grades and comments in Illustration 8-1 are merely given as examples of what pages *might* look like. The teacher could just look over these weekly or periodically and make comments like: "Didn't put in much time this week!" or a simple but enthusiastic:"VERY GOOD!"

In the notebook, the front side of the sheet would be left blank except for the group's number or lesson time. The back side would contain the names of the students in the class with four spaces between each. The front side of the following page (so the two pages will be facing each other when the notebook is open) would contain the book or books being used, lesson assignments, notes as to the discussions that pertain to the lesson, items that should be taken up at the next lessons, or items that could be taken up in the technic class.

The page containing the students' names would be set up thusly:

1st   line—the student's name
2nd line—Absences would be recorded here. All would be
                needed is the entering of the date, i.e., if the child

ILLUSTRATION 8-1

GROUP IV

Richard Ameduri
10/8   11/2
WF 97

Charles Beno

WF 97

emb

Ted Camesano
10/1   12/2
WF 90

rk

Joseph Maggio

WF 92

Guy Morice

WF 90

Ronald Poccia

WF 92

ILLUSTRATION 8-1—continued

First Division Band Method II
Breeze-Easy Recital Pieces

9/10 p3 Solo #29
      pattern of a scale

9/17 p4

9/24 p5
      Compare beat with
      water hose.

10/1 p6   Solo #30
      ways of stopping a tone

was absent October 12, November 3, and December 10, the second line would contain: 10/12, 11/3 and 12/10.

3rd line—would be for grades. There is not sufficient room for grading every lesson on this compact form but periodically a grade should be given. If the *Watkins-Farnum Performance Scale* is given, the entry would contain a code letter like: "W-F" and then followed by the grade. If a playing test were given at a particular point in the semester the entry would be recorded with the letter "P" and then the grade. If this is the first semester of lessons, it might be well to keep a record of what grade each child had gotten on the musical aptitude test. In this case enter a letter "A" for "aptitude" followed by the grade.

4th line —could be used for entering brief notes like: "emb" for "embouchure troubles" or "rh" if the child is having rhythm problems. "D.M." might indicate dirty mouthpiece" "D.R." would equal "dirty reed". "T" would be marked down each time the child has to be spoken to for talking out of turn or a simple "D" for lack of discipline.

Full Sized Notebook (8½ x 11)

The setup would be the same as with the compact form except five spaces would be left between each name if the narrow lined notebook paper is used.

With the 8½ x 11 size notebook paper there would be ample room for:

1st line—absences
2nd line—grades for every lesson
3rd line—weekly practice record
4th and 5th lines—attitudes, excuses, problems, etc.

Illustration 8-2 gives an example of this form that would be very elaborate but very useful. This form could be mimeographed with the dates across the top and the student names left blank.

ILLUSTRATION 8-2

DATES:																						
	Homeroom					Phone					Serial No.											
Attendance																						
Grades																						
Practice																						
Attitudes, etc.																						

	Homeroom					Phone					Serial No.											
Attendance																						
Grades																						
Practice																						
Attitudes, etc.																						

	Homeroom					Phone					Serial No.											
Attendance																						
Grades																						
Practice																						
Attitudes, etc.																						

	Homeroom					Phone					Serial No.											
Attendance																						
Grades																						
Practice																						
Attitudes, etc.																						

	Homeroom					Phone					Serial No.											
Attendance																						
Grades																						
Practice																						
Attitudes, etc.																						

	Homeroom					Phone					Serial No.											
Attendance																						
Grades																						
Practice																						
Attitudes, etc.																						

FILE FOLDER TYPE RECORDS

The same type of form as shown in Illustration 8-2 would be used except that it would be glued (with rubber cement across the top) to the inner left side of a manila file folder. A blank sheet of paper would be glued to the left side of the folder for the purpose of keeping a record of the lesson assignments.

USING A PRACTICE RECORD BOOK

A practice record book like that shown in Illustration 4-4 would be especially appropriate if the class also used this type of record. For the teacher, one book would be designated for each of his classes,the class number being printed on the outside of the cover. Inside the cover would be listed the students in that particular class. In the section designated on the illustration for individual practice record, the teacher would merely print one child's initials in the place where the days of the week are. Thus he would have a spot for recording particulars about each child in the class. In the place for the total day's practice, he could enter the total week's practice for each child or use the space for entering a grade for each week's lesson.

PERMANENT RECORD

A permanent record is especially important if the school system is a 6-3-3 type with different band directors and/or instrumental teachers at each level. This record would be passed on with the children. In this way the children will feel that there is some continuity and it also gives the next teacher information on who he can expect, and who he should expect. With records like these the teacher could easily seek out those who may be on the verge of dropping out of the instrumental program.

There are several companies that publish forms of this type. Illustration 8-3 can be purchased through the local music store from C. G. Conn Ltd. It is a sturdy manila envelope containing space for a wealth of information. Illustration 8-4 is published by G. Leblanc Corporation. This too can be ordered through the local music store.

SCHOOL-OWNED EQUIPMENT

A simple ledger-type sheet would do nicely for recording a list of all school-owned equipment. This should include all equipment except instruments and music. Percussion traps, however , would go on this list. A separate form is necessary for instruments and music. This list should include such items as music stands and how many, electronic devices like a strobotuner, metronome, tape recorder, chairs (if they are assigned specifically to the instrumental department), etc. Each time a new purchase is made the item should be added to this list. The list should include the following information about each item if it is available:

1. serial number
   a. If possible every item should be given a school number if it does not have a serial number
2. from whom the item was purchased
3. the date the item was purchased
4. the requisition number
5. the cost of the item

SCHOOL-OWNED INSTRUMENTS

A fine device for keeping a record of school-owned instruments is a form published by C. G. Conn Ltd. It is called the

ILLUSTRATION 8-3

CONN

MUSIC STUDENT
PERFORMANCE FILE

Name _____ Grade _____
School _____
Instrument _____

NAME _____
ADDRESS _____ PARENT _____
     PHONE _____ AGE _____
MAJOR INSTRUMENT _____ SCHOOL INSTRUMENT? _____ MAKE _____ FINISH _____ SERIAL NO. _____
MISCELLANEOUS _____ MINOR INSTRUMENT _____
UNIFORM: OUT? _____ IN? _____ COAT _____ CAPE _____ SKIRT _____ TROUSERS _____ HAT _____
EXTRA EQUIPMENT _____
INSTRUMENT RACK NO. _____ UNIFORM LOCKER NO. _____ MUSIC FOLDER NO. _____

ORGANIZATION   FREE PERIODS

1ST BAND	MON.	1 - 2 - 3 - 4 - 5 - 6 - 7 - 8
2ND BAND	TUES.	1 - 2 - 3 - 4 - 5 - 6 - 7 - 8
BEGINNER'S BAND	WED.	1 - 2 - 3 - 4 - 5 - 6 - 7 - 8
1ST ORCHESTRA	THURS.	1 - 2 - 3 - 4 - 5 - 6 - 7 - 8
2ND ORCHESTRA	FRI.	1 - 2 - 3 - 4 - 5 - 6 - 7 - 8
STRING BEGINNER		
MAJORETTE		

ORGANIZATIONAL OFFICER _____
FESTIVAL RATINGS AND AWARDS _____

MUSICIAN 1ST CLASS _____ MUSICIAN 2ND CLASS _____ MUSICIAN 3RD CLASS _____
PRIVATE INSTRUCTION? _____ TEACHER _____
ADDITIONAL INFORMATION _____

ILLUSTRATION 8-4

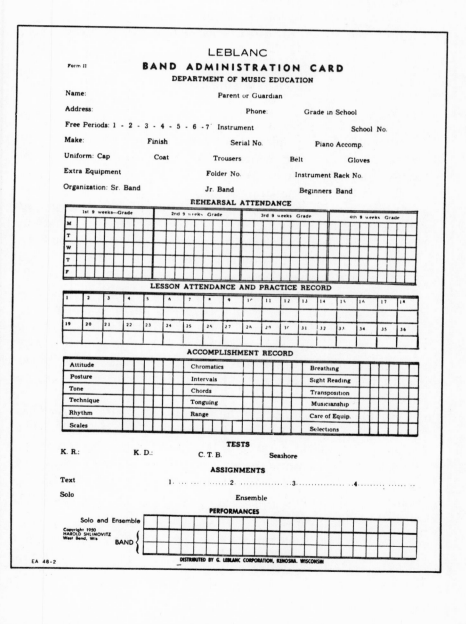

School Band Inventory and Depreciation Record (see Illustration 8-5). This comes with an explanation as to how to carry on a businesslike management system for band instruments.

There must also be a record of who is using which instrument. Illustrations 8-6 and 8-7[1] are some examples of this type form that could be mimeographed. Illustration 8-8 is a professionally prepared inventory system that makes an excellent and professional record of instruments in the school's inventory.

SCHOOL-OWNED MUSIC

A steel file cabinet must be provided for the storage of all band music. Each arrangement should be stored in a manila envelope. Because most elementary band libraries are not too extensive, the following setup should suffice.

Place the music in a drawer and give the drawer a letter. The first drawer will be designated as drawer "A". The second drawer would be designated as drawer "B", etc. The first envelope in drawer "A" would be number "A-1", the second envelope in drawer "A" would be numbered "A-2", etc. Likewise the first envelope in drawer "B" would be numbered "B-1." The 15th envelope in drawer "C" would be number "C-15."

A file card (3" x 5") should be made out for each composition. File cards can be made out with the title first, with the author first or with the subject listed first. For a small library perhaps a title card is all that is needed. By placing the drawer and envelope number on the file card each composition can be located easily.

All the music owned by the school should also be listed on an inventory sheet. A ledger-type sheet will suffice for this also. This music inventory can also be of help to the director when he is looking for music for his next program. Here within easy glance is a list of all the compositions in the library. This inventory sheet should also carry the drawer and envelope number of each composition.

---

[1]"Inventory Records for Musical Instruments," *The New York State School Music News,* XXVII, 9, (May-June 1964), 30.

ILLUSTRATION 8-5

REPAIR RECORD OF_____ Sousaphone   Victory   100123
                        INSTRUMENT   MAKE   SERIAL NUMBER

	DESCRIPTION OF REPAIR	REPAIRED BY	DATE	COST
1.	Repair damage to bell - cleaning	A.B. Music Shop	6/15/46	$ 40.00
2.	Complete rebuilding, valves refitted	Thomas & Griffin	6/25/51	150.00
3.	Cleaning, adjusting, dents removed	" " "	6/4/55	100.00
4.				
5.				
6.				
7.				
8.				
9.				
10.				
11.				

ILLUSTRATION 8-5—continued

Band Instrument Inventory and Depreciation Record

Name of Instrument ___Sousaphone___ Make ___Victory___ Model __BBb__ Finish _2_ Serial _100123_

From Whom Purchased _____Lyric Music Store_____ Date ___Oct. 1___ 19_41_

COST RECORD

COST, REPAIRS & REPLACEMENTS	MO.	DAY	YR.	EXPENSE	ACCUMULATED COST
Acquisition	6	10	41		400 00
Repairs (5th year)	6	15	46	40 00	440 00
Complete Overhaul (rebuilding)(10th yr.)	6	25	51	150 00	590 00
Cleaning and Valve Adjustment, Dents	6	4	55	100 00	690 00
Removed (14th year)					

DEPRECIATION RECORD

YR.	DEPRECIATION RATE %	NET ANNUAL RESERVE	ACCUMULATED RESERVE FUND	NET BOOK VALUATION	APPRAISAL	
					VALUE	DATE
1	25%	100 00	100 00	300 00		
2	13%	52 00	152 00	248 00		
3	12%	48 00	200 00	200 00		
4	8%	32 00	232 00	168 00		
5	8%	35 20	267 20	172 80		
6	7%	30 80	298 00	142 00		
7	7%	30 80	328 80	111 20		
8	7%	30 80	359 60	80 40		
9	7%	30 80	390 40	49 60		
10	6%	35 40	425 80	14 20		
	100%					
11		32 85	458 65	131 35		
12		32 84	491 49	98 51		
13		32 84	524 33	65 67		
14		82 84	607 17	82 83		
15		82 83	690 00	0		
16						
17						
18						
19						
20						

Estimated Life Expectancy of Instrument as Result of Repairs ___5___

ILLUSTRATION 8-6

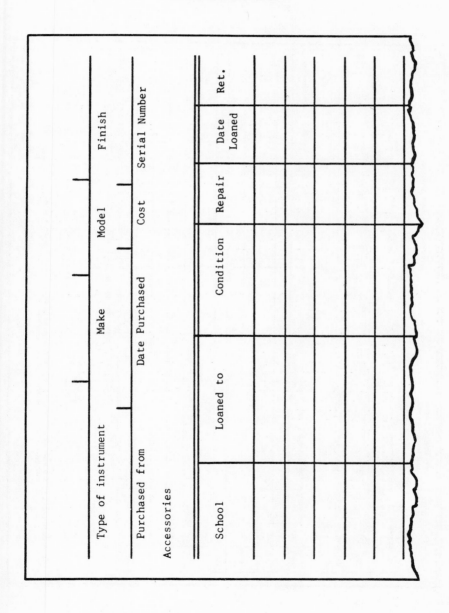

ILLUSTRATION 8-7

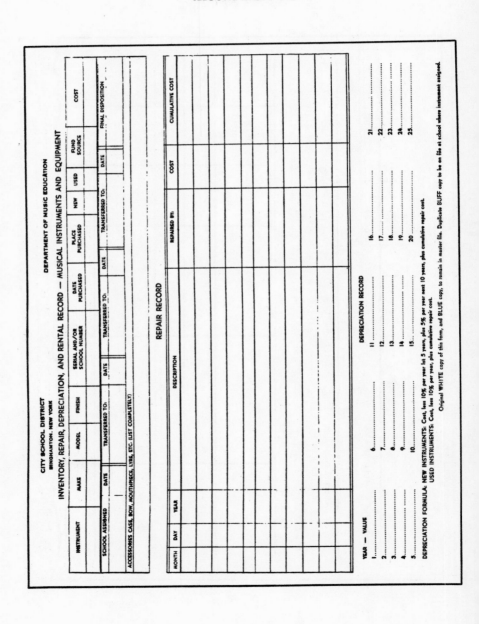

ILLUSTRATION 8-7—continued

ILLUSTRATION 8-8

Iorio Pupil Controls, 220 Shell St., Harrisburg, Pa.

INSTRUMENT INVENTORY RECORD

DATE ISSUED	STUDENT'S NAME	ADDRESS	SCHOOL	CONDITION	RENTAL PD. I SEM.	RENTAL PD. II SEM.	DATE RETURNED

INSTRUMENT PROPERTY OF _____ BOUGHT BY _____

INVENTORY NUMBER	INSTRUMENT	DESCRIPTION	SERIAL NUMBER	COST	INSURED VALUE	DATE PURCHASED	PLACE PURCHASED

Coda

Efficiency and professionalism are the key words in any endeavor. So too in the management of a band program. Efficiency allows one to make wise use of the time available. It allows one (in the case of an elementary band program) to spend more time with the children teaching them the inwards of the music.

Efficiency starts with a knowledge of those things one must do and the order in which they must be done.

In the first steps toward carrying on an efficient elementary band program make out a curriculum. It need not be an elaborate one but may simply be a list of books to be used throughout the elementary years for each instrument. If one could list along with these books the various techniques to be acquired for each year so much the better. Include in this list the steps to be used in the first few lessons like those shown in Chapter II under "Outline for teaching the clarinet to beginners." The following is a list of items that could be discussed in regard to the learning situation in a complete curriculum outline:

I. Level of learning
   A. Description of the course
   B. General objectives
   C. Materials for the course
   D. Outline of topics
     1. Sequence
     2. Time allocations

E. Sub-units

    1. Topic title   4. Developmental activities

    2. Importance   5. Culminating activities

    3. Specific objectives

The "sub-units" under *E* could simply list representative solos that would be performed by the students for each semester of development. Here too could be listed the various topics to be discussed in the technic classes ((Chapter 4).

Record keeping is usually shunned whenever possible as being of little real value to the instrumentalists. Yet paper work can prove to be a great benefit to overall program. Paper work, if properly designed for efficiency lets all persons involved—the principal, the classroom teacher, the parents and the children know just what is going on and when. A well worked-out curriculum placed in a theme notebook cover and given to the principal gives him an indication that you are more than just a recreational officer letting the kids have fun blowing. It automatically gives the instrumental program some degree of respectability. Most important of all, it lets the teacher know where he is at all times and where he should be going and toward what goals he is trying to lead his instrumentalists.

Following is a check list that might be followed. Several items could be started before the school doors open for classes in September.

    ————Establish a curriculum

    ————Have some extra copies of the curriculum made so they may be filed in the offices of administrators

    ————Set the music library in order (See Chapter 8)

    ————Establish an inventory device for equipment (See Chapter 8)

    ————Establish an inventory device for instruments (See Illustrations 8-5 through 8-8)

    ————Order materials needed that are listed on the "Recruitment Schedule Sheet" (Illustration 1-6)

    ————Set up a form for keeping class records (Illustrations 8-1 or 8-2)

    ————Work out dates called for on the "Recruitment Schedule Sheet"

————Mimeograph recruiting letter (See Illustrations 1-2 through 1-5)

————Mimeograph follow up letters (See Illustrations 5-1 and 5-2)

————Prepare materials for follow up talk to parents (Chapter 5)

————Mimeograph testing materials (Illustration 5-12 through 5-14)

————Establish a reporting device (Illustrations 5-4 through 5-6) and 5-8 through 5-11)

PROFESSIONALISM

Professionalism is best acquired by keeping up on all the latest technics and materials. This is done by attending clinics and conventions of area and national music associations and reading the many fine music periodicals that are being published.

Professionalism can also be shown in much the same way as we discussed the effects of posture on an individual's attitude when playing his instrument. Looking like a professional goes a long way toward being accepted and recognized as a professional. The A-number-one way is by dressing like one. A casual, sloppy band director usually leads to a casual, sloppy band. The band director need not be dressed like he just stepped out of a magazine ad but he should be dressed neatly with a clean suit and wear a tie each day. The presence of his instrument is also a mark of a really professional instrumental teacher. Have the instrument ready to play and demonstrate to the children how a particular section of the music is to be played. If private lessons are to be given one should be prepared to show students how various passages must be played. Needless to say it should always be in top working condition, clean and always handled with the utmost of care and respect. Psychologists are constantly saying to adults: Be an example to the youth. The band director too must be an example for the students will merely reflect him and his attitudes.

Index

A

B